CW01646663

The photograph of Priaulx Rainier on the front cover was taken in 1967. The score is from *Quanta*.

'COME AND LISTEN TO THE STARS SINGING'

Priaulx at Bryanston summer school.

'Come and Listen to the Stars Singing'
Priaulx Rainier: A Pictorial Biography

June Opie

Alison Hodge
1988

First published in 1988 by
Alison Hodge, Bosulval, Newmill, Penzance, Cornwall TR20 8XA

© June Opie, 1988

Designer Stuart Hamilton

No part of this publication may be reproduced or transmitted in any form or by any means without the permission in writing of the publishers.

ISBN 0 906720 17 6

Typesetting by TNR Productions Ltd., 19 Westbourne Road, London N7 8AN
Origination, printing and binding by LR Printing Services, Crawley

For Shirley and Desmond

My knowledge of Priaulx Rainier's early years is based entirely on what she, or her sister, told me: and that of the first half of her musical and adult life on what she, or her friends, told me. Sources have been acknowledged. *J.O.*

Contents

1. The Drakensberg foothills.

Early Years

Images of Africa

The vast spaces
The immense silence – which becomes an almost
  audible presence
The night sky ablaze with stars
The blue mountains, with their streams and
  aromatic herbal scents
Sounds travelling in crystal-clear air from great
  distances
The cries of birds and beasts,
  and
The haunting, long drawn out liquid syllables of
  Zulu, calling from the hills.

P.R.

PRIAULX RAINIER was born on 3 February 1903, at Howick, Natal, South Africa where an immense reach of land spreads from the foothills of the Drakensberg Mountains and falls eastward towards the sea. Little is known of her parents. Her mother was a Howard, the Howard men of naval tradition as were the Rainiers; the Howards were English, the Rainiers Huguenot in origin, claiming descent from Charlemagne. Both parents were born in England, but all their married life lived in Africa where the children were born. Fourth in a family of five, Priaulx spent the first ten years of her life on the borders of Zululand, around her the great space of Africa, its high arc of sky unbroken by clouds, at night heavy with stars. Below lay a sweep of grass-covered hills, green in the rains of summer, bleached pale biscuit in the frosty winter sun and, behind, the range of the Drakensbergs, sometimes snow-covered but a burning blue all summer.

2. Priaulx's mother, Ellen Rainier, *c.* 1914–20.

3. Priaulx (*right*) at 12 or 13; her sister, Yollande, and Uncle Arthur.

From an early age she was attentive to the sounds of wildlife about her: the rustle of a snake in the grass, the call of a baboon. In summer dramatic thunderstorms sometimes lasted days and nights: electric storms which sent flashes of lightning across the clouds hanging over the hills below, followed by hailstorms that could be heard approaching from miles away. They produced a crescendo of noise, finally battering on the galvanized roof, the only roofing able to withstand the attack. No spoken word could be heard until they were over, and then every leaf and every fruit was found stripped from the trees and bushes by the hailstones.

Sensitive to atmospheric pressure, Priaulx felt the approach of thunderstorms and developed severe headaches: it was as if the world was pressing in on her. Sometimes she became quite ill and her mother, despite the other children and a great many duties to attend to, recognizing that the pysically strong child had a rare gift and a sensitivity that required nurturing, would lie her in quietness on a sofa, make a broth which she particularly liked and feed it gently to her.

Business necessitated her father's frequent absence from home, and his return was always a time for rejoicing. The children could see him from far off and, wild with excitement, would run to meet him, their mother waiting at the gate. Almost before his horse had stopped its gallop he would leap down and sweep the children, in turn, into his arms in an embrace that lifted them off the ground. Then it was their mother's turn. Then Buller's – he was the family dog who alerted them to their father's approach. He would stand quietly beside their mother waiting for

4. 'Processions like these used to pass our door.'

his welcome, as much a part of their lives as every other member of the family, there to attack rats and snakes and to protect their mother from any untoward intrusion, man or beast. Priaulx adored him.

Some two or three miles away was a large wattle plantation where a thousand Hindus, brought from India, lived and worked. Their festivities were held at the appropriate times, with traditional music, but the days before were filled with the beatings of tom-toms, unceasing night and day . . . This experience of the tom-toms at an early age, the excitement, the mystery and the frenzied working up to climaxes which then dropped to a threatening murmur, never left Priaulx. Nor did the tones of the Zulus calling, or the ever-present sounds of nature.

To add to her awareness and aural sensitivity the piano sounded four or five hours a day as her two older sisters, both dedicated musicians, practised. The classical repertoire for the instrument was in her ears and mind from her cradle – literally so. It was her sister Nella, eleven years older, who discovered that when

5. **Priaulx's sister, Nella.**

6. **Headlands at the Cape.**

both practising and caring for Priaulx as a baby she had only to pull her against the wood of the piano and whatever protestations had begun would cease. As Priaulx began to crawl, she placed herself under the keyboard with her back up against the piano – it became a favourite position and pastime.

Buller also loved the sound, particularly Schumann's 'Carnival', and whenever the girls played it, he took up a position beside the piano and howled. This was soon recognized as singing and it became a concert performance. When they had visitors one of the girls was chosen to play the piece and Buller sang, refining his performance by sitting with his back to the piano in order to face his audience. It was astonishing, people applauded and it finally reached a stage where Buller would come in and worry their mother until he was allowed to perform, receive his applause and go to each guest in turn to be patted on the head.

Nella had almost sole charge of Priaulx when she was a very young child and would often take her outside, away from the house, to a huge tree where Nella herself had peace and quiet in which to read. If Priaulx became restless she would read aloud. In addition to the piano Priaulx was given very early experience of the excellence of the English language, for Nella was a most selective reader. Nella and Peter, the two oldest children, were closest to Priaulx. It was Peter who taught her to ride bareback, swim, climb and explore. Finding herself always in competition with boys, Priaulx developed an endurance and physical strength beyond most girls, and a fierce competitiveness.

7. **On the beach.**

8. **With their white Persian.**

9. **The only photograph of Priaulx playing the violin.**

Unlike her sisters, when the time came for her to learn the piano she showed little success at it and, because of this, was given a three-quarter size violin. Her gift was astonishingly and immediately apparent.

It was decided that the family must move to Cape Town in order to give the girls a proper musical education. This meant living by the sea. It was Priaulx's first experience of it, a new excitement in her life, the feel of it, its rhythms and sounds. The views she found from places like Sea Point and Botany Bay stirred within her a desire she was unable to explain. She roamed the foothills of Table Mountain with Peter, fell in love with the proteas, and the leucadendrons – especially the silver tree which grows wild there, nowhere else in the world.

Priaulx was ten years old when they moved to the Cape. She was entered as a violin student at the newly-established College of Music in Cape Town under the principalship of W.H. Bell. This proved to be the richest and most important part of her musical education. Under Bell's guidance she was quartet playing from the age of eleven, and did so regularly. Her attendance at symphony concerts provided a new assault in sound upon her ears. Bell was a remarkable man, open to every branch of the arts – music, drama and literature – and a great innovator. His influence upon her was lasting.

10. Winifred Katzin.

11. Miss A.E.F. Horniman.

Also at the Cape she met another person who was to make a deep impression on her young, eager mind – not a musician, but a woman of quite remarkable comprehension and intellect – Winifred Katzin. Her awareness and understanding of human values, and of the truth that lies behind them, was a central force in the development of Priaulx's mind foı the rest of her life.

In 1920 Priaulx won the University of South Africa Overseas Scholarship which was to take her to England to study violin at the Royal Academy of Music, away from her country, her parents, her beloved Nella and adored Peter. It had been arranged that in England she would be met by Miss A.E.F. Horniman as her sister Nella had been before her. Miss Horniman, celebrated for her work in the theatre, was a supporter of the Abbey Theatre in Dublin, creator of the first repertory theatre in Manchester, friend of W.B. Yeats and Bernard Shaw.

When she got off the boat-train at Victoria Priaulx did not know what to do. She stood on the platform with her suitcases, lost, wondering where to go next. There were only two people left on the platform; she was one, the other was a tall, straight figure in a huge cape pacing up and down. The figure suddenly swooped towards

12. On the Wiltshire downs.

13. Priaulx, soon after her arrival in England.

her: it was Miss Horniman. As Priaulx was about to pick up her suitcases, Miss Horniman summoned a porter and, with considerable authority, commanded him to take them to the left luggage department were a man would call for them later. Priaulx was transfixed. That meeting was her meeting with Europe.

Miss Horniman had planned to take her on a grand tour. But first there was an invitation to visit Stratford-upon-Avon for some ten days of theatre-going. Here they met and dined several times with Bernard Shaw, occasions when Priaulx said little, simply listening to the brilliant conversation – occasions she was never to forget.

Then the tour. Miss Horniman took her to France, Italy, Germany – everywhere that art and literature had flourished for centuries. The young scholarship student, her mind fresh from the spaces and wilderness of Africa, who had seen Zulu processions celebrating tribal events pass her door, was shown processions of ancient Greeks caught in sculpted friezes in their celebrations of war, their sacrifices, their gods; shown the galleries, the architecture, and introduced to the works of great composers played by some of the finest musicians in the world. With an imagination eager for stimulus, and a mind able to absorb everything she was being led towards, it was a tour she remembered in detail all her life, and an enrichment for which she was forever grateful.

14. Peter Rainier in South America.

15. Peter's children (with Indian nursemaid) on the two-day ride.

16. The copper horn.

By this time Nella had taken a teaching post at University College, Cape Town. Peter, who had developed into a fine linguist – as had a sister, Yollande – had settled, after various adventures, in the high mountains of South America in charge of the emerald mines at Bogotá. He wrote Priaulx fascinating accounts of his life there (he was later to become an author); he had married, built his own house and had children, another Peter and two daughters. The place was so isolated it was a two-day horse ride for the children to meet their mother on her return from the nearest town. Photographs accompanied his letters – of the house, the children, the mountains – and once of a magnificent copper horn he had found on a mine. Priaulx mounted this photograph and put it on one side of a pigeon-hole inside her working desk where she could see it whenever she opened it.

17. In Europe.

18. Nella (*left*).

19. Aubrey Rainier, aged 7.

20. King Proteas on Table Mountain.

She wrote to Peter, to Nella and the family, pouring out hundreds of words, keeping herself vital and loving to them, and they to her, particularly Nella. During this time a cousin, Aubrey Rainier, exhibiting the family gift for music came, at the age of eight, to give a cello recital at the Wigmore Hall. The programme notice read:

AUBREY RAINIER – THE EIGHT-YEAR-OLD CELLIST – PIANOFORTE – GERALD MOORE.
Tickets (including Tax) 3/-

Priaulx's studies at the Royal Academy of Music, begun after her tour with Miss Horniman, continued and life, so different from the one she had known as a child, deluged her with new experiences as she came to explore London. Miss Horniman had taught her the grid system on which London streets operate so that she could find her way about more easily.

During her studentship at the RAM she paid one brief visit to South Africa. It was to be her last for fifty years. In the knowledge of all she had learned in Europe, of music, drama, art and literature it made a very deep impression on her, and it was after this visit that she felt her first impulse to compose.

Musical Life in London

RETURNING TO ENGLAND Priaulx settled permanently in London. The idea that had occurred to her, when she felt that first impulse to compose, took the form of a movement for string quartet. She was not a composition student but felt compelled to try. The resulting piece was in 5/8 time and ended on a discord. It was written in 1924!

In 1925 she was offered a post teaching violin and aural training at the Badminton School, Bristol – a school which Indira Gandi attended. It had a high standard of achievement, particularly in music. Circumstances demanded that she earn a living as a teacher and violinist so there was little time for composing; but there were wonderful moments for she frequently played quartets and quintets with other gifted players. One of these, who led the quartets, was the brilliant violinist Orrea Pernel. Playing frequently together they became close friends and learned much from each other in interpretation and technique.

For some time Priaulx had been going to Gunby Hall, in Spilsby, at the request of Lady Diana Massingberd, herself a fine musician, who invited small groups of players for weekends, for the sheer enjoyment of performing together. They became great friends and Priaulx introduced Orrea Pernel to her. From that time on they would often play together at the Hall. On one visit, because she had been delayed in London by another commitment, Priaulx arrived at the local railway station very late and in the dark, to find that the chauffeur had been sent to collect her. Driving back to the Hall the car skidded badly on a corner because the chauffeur, experienced and careful as he was, could not see that ice had formed across the road. They overturned. Priaulx was thrown head first into the windscreen, and her head was opened to the skull. She was taken immediately to the cottage hospital nearby and was treated there, Lady Massingberd insisting that her long hair was not cut off.

21. Orrea Pernel.

She was unable to play for six months after the accident and began composing again, writing a duet for violin and piano. When Orrea Pernel saw it she decided to include the work in her forthcoming recital, with Harriet Cohen, at the Wigmore Hall. She encouraged Priaulx to begin composing seriously. A small grant was offered to her for composition and she wrote *Three Greek Epigrams*, the Piano *Étude* and the String Quartet. She had no composition lessons and, except for encouragement from Arnold Bax, who had seen the student quartet, she worked on her own, developing a very sharp critical sense towards her own work.

Feeling the need for further comment she took the works to Nadia Boulanger, master teacher, in Paris, to try to find what direction her work should take in the future. After seeing what Priaulx had done Mademoiselle Boulanger agreed to

22. (*L. to r.*) **Orrea, Priaulx, James Brock and David Morse in France.**

23. Gunby Hall.

24. On holiday.

accept her for discussion lessons. During the two and a half months she was there, she did no actual composition. What Mademoiselle did ask was that she write something every morning, as soon as she got up, and bring it to her. This Priaulx found extremely difficult, not liking to write under that kind of pressure, wanting more time to think about the music before committing it to paper, but Mademoiselle insisted. It was an intense period of great value and stimulus, and turning up the exercises forty years later, Priaulx was surprised at what she had written.

In Paris Priaulx met again the poet David Gascoyne who expressed a wish to write a poem with words suitable for singing, for her to set to music. *Requiem* resulted. Because he had been a chorister at Salisbury Cathedral, David Gascoyne chose words suitable for singing and designated verses for voice and chorus, dividing the poem into three parts, so that the musical structure was already established. It was 1937. The Second World War was yet to come, but the words of the poem were prophetic – presaging the holocaust that was to descend, destroying hopes and ideals – and appealing to mysterious, unknown forces for strength and guidance.

When she returned to London Orrea Pernel, who had been waiting to hear the *Three Greek Epigrams*, suggested that as Priaulx had no piano in her room, she should have a small party of friends in the music room at her flat, where she would play the accompaniment for the *Epigrams* if a singer could be found. This was not easy because the music was original; so original it was considered very difficult. The eventual singer Miette Muthesius explained:

> No-one could be found who *dared*! So Orrea brought me the songs and asked me to try and sing them. I found them fascinating and extremely difficult, especially the second one. I agreed. I was quite petrified at first because I knew no-one, except Orrea who accompanied me. I think I was a bit wobbly at first, but it gradually got better.
>
> Priaulx was extremely nice and very grateful . . . She had now a good idea of what was passable, and what needed working on. She offered to coach me, which I was naturally only too glad to accept and this resulted in my singing the songs at various important houses.

25. Miette Muthesius, 1933.

26. Timothy Baxter, while studying with Priaulx, and now Professor of Composition at the RAM.

It also resulted in a lifelong friendship which Priaulx treasured. Beautiful Miette, travelling in and out of Europe, knew so much about the cultural interchange between nations and, of course, there was always music to discuss – its interpretations and its challenges.

Just as Priaulx was beginning to establish herself as a composer of promise, war broke out. Contemporary concerts in London ceased for a while, and all chance of a performance of the Quartet seemed to disappear. As the war continued everyone's life was disrupted and disorganized, often disastrously, but because of the reputation she had earned as a teacher of exceptional qualities, Priaulx was appointed Professor of Composition at the Royal Academy of Music. Like everyone else she was obliged to live and work under very austere conditions. Timothy Baxter, who studied under her, recalled that:

> her room at the Academy was cold, bare, and had one pane of glass missing – covered over with cardboard – but Priaulx made it quite different. What she had to say about one's work, the ease with which she saw everything and clarified it, her mere presence made the room not what it was.

27. Forking hay.

28. With Pola Nirenska (*left*) in Europe.

29. Pola Nirenska.

She gave all she could to those who came to her for encouragement, yet returning one day to her flat she wrote in her diary:

> In this bitter windless cold – so cold that out of doors it slowly seeps through clothing like icy water, the mind turned within itself has no warmth left to externalise.

She became an air raid warden in the Kensington area where she lived, and on vacation from the RAM went as part of the war effort to help on the land, harvesting in Hertfordshire – working farm horses, forking hay – hard physical tasks, competing with whatever men were left. There she met the sculptor Henry Moore, and was invited to visit his studio. Priaulx listened while he talked, of the sources he drew on and of the critical eye of a creative artist.

A passionate person, Priaulx was drawn towards many altars, none more strongly than dance. She loved movement, rhythm, the tenderness and fire in the physical expression of the body during dance. Her comprehension of movement had grown out of her early days in Africa, a response to the instinctual, sensuous flow of bodies: a response instinctive in itself. Passages in her music could be as pointed and exact as a dancer's foot, the movements as controlled and full of meaning. Not surprisingly, she was attracted to dancers. One of these was Pola Nirenska, and their friendship culminated in Priaulx going to live with Pola and her husband Jan Karski, writer and historian. She attended all Nirenska's recitals and became deeply involved – as she always did with friends – in every aspect of the performance. She loved to watch dance and was attentive to every detail, her mind a mosaic of images which could expand and contract, change form and colour, depending upon the stimulus presented to them – not ordinary reactions. She was not ordinary in any sense of the word. She was a person of vision, but not of hypothesis.

Dec 28 Good Lord! — The most glorious winter's day – bright sunshine – brilliant light – a freezing East wind not too hard AND — my first race at the helm in Zephyr this morning! It was so freezing I couldn't hold anything getting boat ready. Zephyr after being last over line (of fast boats) overtook all except Venturia and passed her round the Buoy! Owing to the latter getting in irons at that moment, we fouled her at the buoy so withdrew

39

from the Race but ran ahead until requested to stand aside by V. We could have beaten her otherwise! Imagine! my first race overlap. Venturia who had on the run up at least 200 yds start! There was a lot of wind too & I handled "Dart" & passed her most successfully before she could luff me. Terribly exciting race passing boat after boat! When I can sail her properly & have a trained crew I have a good chance of making a good race for V. MUST learn from now on to sail on mainsail. My confidence increased enormously because I forgot my fears when racing & trying to sail hard close whatever may. It is the most thrilling game! to outmanoeuvre by wits! forethought! judgement! I cannot recover from my astonishment! To Pass Venturia! First race!! Everyone so pleased & friendly & encouraging. I took a line of my own too – didn't just follow V.

Dec 30 Sent letter [30] to Nella. In bed with mild flu these 2 days. Much better tonight. Food so difficult – Lived on tinned milk (my 3 milkless days would amuse now!) tin of celery soup. Weak tea, hot water, with a very old piece of home dried orange peel for

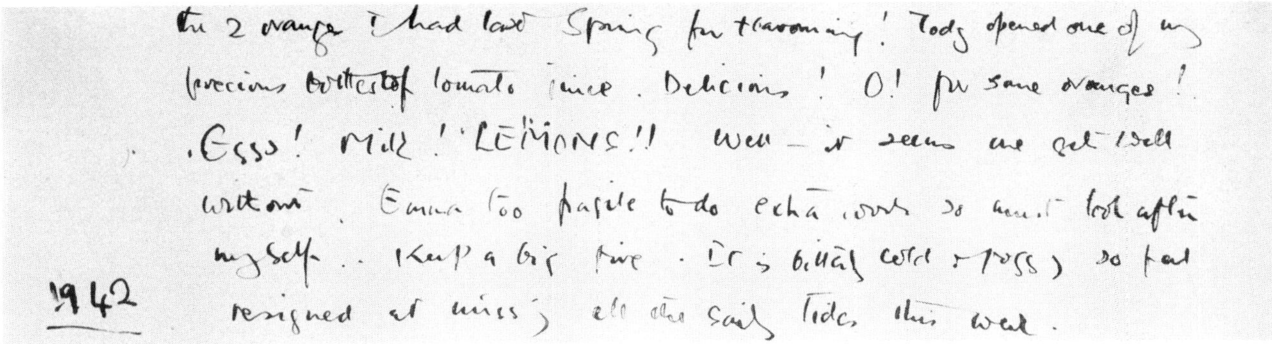
1942

the 2 oranges I had last Spring for flavouring! Today opened one of my precious bottles of tomato juice. Delicious! O! for some oranges! Eggs! Milk! LEMONS!! Well – it seems we get well without. Emma too fragile to do extra work so must look after myself.. Keep a big fire. It is bitterly cold & foggy so feel resigned at missing all the sailing tides this week.

30. From Priaulx's diary, 1941.

To her delight Priaulx was, at this time, given the opportunity to sail; not often, but enough to feel the waves and the wind, and the sea-blood of a long line of naval captains and admirals from whom she was descended. Entries in her diary in the winter of 1941 reflect her enthusiasm for this pastime:

> [December 28] Good Lord! The most glorious winter's day – bright sunshine – brilliant light – a freezing East wind not too hard AND my first race at the helm in Zephyr this morning! It was freezing couldn't hold anything getting boat ready. Zephyr after being last over the line (of fast boats) overtook *all* except Ventenia and past her round the buoy! Owing to the latter getting in irons at that moment, we fouled her and the buoy, so withdrew from the Race but ran ahead until requested to stand aside by V. We could have beaten her otherwise! Imagine! My first race overtaking Ventenia who had, on run up, at least 200 yards start! There was a lot of wind too and I blanketed "Dart" and passed her most successfully before she could luff me. Terribly exciting race passing boat after boat! *When* I can sail her properly and have a trained crew I have a good chance of making a good race for V. *MUST* learn from now on to sail on main sail. My confidence increased enormously because I forget my fears when racing and try to sail hard come what may. It is the most thrilling game! To outmanoeuvre by wits! Forethought! Judgement! I cannot recover from my astonishment! To pass Ventenia! First race!! Everyone so pleased and friendly and encouraging. I took a line of my own too – didn't just follow V.
>
> [December 30] Sent letter 30 to Nella. In bed with mild flu these two days. Much better tonight. Food is so difficult. Lived on tinned milk (my three milkless days *would* occur now!). Tin of celery soup. Weak tea. Hot water with a very old piece of dried orange peel from the two oranges I had last spring for flavouring. Today opened one of my precious bottles of tomato juice. Delicious! Oh! For some oranges! Eggs! Milk! LEMONS! Well – it seems we get well without. Emma too fragile to do extra work so must look after myself. Keep a big fire. It is bitterly cold and foggy so feel resigned at missing all sailing tides this week.

In London Priaulx cycled everywhere, undaunted by crater holes left by a night's bombing, or danger from falling masonry; pedalling to the Academy, to the famous lunch-time concerts of classical music if she had time, and cycling with friends, especially the painters John Craxton and Lucian Freud. Musicians and artists grew closer to one another as they struggled to preserve the ideals and values they upheld against the horrors and the slaughter, the waste of if all, and the scale of destruction as the war continued. But the war also brought Priaulx the unexpected friendship of people she would not otherwise have known, and demonstrated people's willingness to help each other. This moved her deeply and she wrote of it in her diary in 1942:

> A truly terrible two years have turned into peaceful deep waters, where though my deepest emotional life is at a standstill, friends are with me though I do not know them well. Some quality of the spirit I have not yet experienced lies between us. If the War ceased there would be yet another turmoil for which I am not yet ready or strong enough . . .

By now she had joined a coterie of musicians, painters and writers who gathered together during the war. Among them were Arthur Waley, the poet and Chinese scholar; the writer Elias Canetti, who had come from Vienna; Michael Tippett and William Glock, who became her close friends. Michael Tippett gave a series of concerts at Morley College with its choir and *ad hoc* orchestra. Such were the relationships of the group that on one occasion Benjamin Britten and Peter Pears were to be seen singing in the choir for a performance of Purcell.

In 1944 came the first public performances of Priaulx's Quartet at the Gerald Cooper concerts in the Wigmore Hall, and the National Gallery Concerts. After a private performance of the Quartet in 1940, William Glock writing in the *Observer* concluded:

> it has countless touches that leave no doubt as to the talent that created it. I cannot recommend this work too strongly to enterprising string quartets. It is emotionally satisfying, technically challenging, certain and precise in all its calculations; and I think audiences all over the country would enjoy it . . .

31. **Michael Tippett.**

32. **Nella**

That same year, after she had finished the Suite for Clarinet and Piano, Priaulx was asked to write music for a new propaganda film using percussion only. This was a new and strange experience. The music for the film, called *Fire in Our Factory*, was recorded by the Blades brothers. She described it graphically in a letter to her sister Nella:

7th October, 1944

Darling Nella,

A letter to you is long overdue. I was horrified to find under a pile of notes for the film music a long aerogram in two sections, never posted. I apologise – not usually bad in that way. I don't know what it is, but the mental fatigue everyone is suffering from is quite indescribable these days – I suppose War strain. I feel sometimes I can't go on another minute and yet I cannot relax and try and rest . . .

Thank you for sending another parcel. Nothing has arrived since my last acknowledgement. I am very fond of candied peel in whole pieces. One so craves for citrus flavours.

Atmosphere pressure affects me abominably I have always known that. I learn that some humans are so sensitive or allergic to it that they have (in Siberia for instance where exhaustive tests are made) discovered some people to be taken really ill 3 days before the most sensitive instruments known have registered a fall in the barometer announcing an electric storm . . .

I hope young Peter [nephew] will cross my path before long. How charming of the young man to write to you, your stock must be very high with Peter [brother] to have shown the boy what you mean to him and obviously what he must mean to you.

I have just finished 2 of the most appalling weeks work. Last Monday week the film unit was informed that the Ministry of Aircraft Production was interested in our film – wanted to show it to heads of Fire Services, Industry, Cabinet Ministers, etc., this week – but they wanted some scenes altered. Ensued a terrible lot of work – re-shooting – me rewriting score. Because of re-recording had the opportunity to make a better job of it. I wasn't happy about the first recording, lack of experience and inefficient drummer caused a lot of notes in the sound. For 2 days I sat on the telephone trying to find a timpanist free – one who could also play percussion. The score was arranged for one pair who had to be pretty nippy, but the trouble is that good Rumba-band players can handle 2,000 instruments at once but scarcely any can read a score, mostly improvising. Finally I got someone for the recording on Friday. Next morning, Friday recording was cancelled to Monday afternoon! Drummer had a date! So the fun started all over again! Finally I got Jimmy Blades a Lancashire man the best percussionist in London and he wanted to see the score and go through it with me at 10 on Monday at the BBC studios, Maida Vale. On Saturday Pola had a Dance Recital so there was an awful lot to do. I see after her costumes on those occasions . . .

Blades phoned asking to make sure of a second score so I sat up to 3.30 a.m. copying one extra. He wanted to have it by him all day. Next morning dashed to Maida Vale. Found him a little man with burning blue eyes . . . heaving tymps about. We went into the big studio where was ranged a vast collection of percussion instruments he was using at the rehearsal for a 2 o'clock broadcast with Ronald Biggs. We went through the score – he shaking his head at the changes of sticks. "Now lass" he said "I'll be straight with you, I can't undertake to do it justice alone – it's wonderful stuff but the changes are too tricky for recording – I'll bung it up!! My brother is coming down in a while

– it'll cost you another 3 guineas but we'll get it all in no fuss and bother at the time". All this was said in broadest Lancashire. I could only accept . . .

I lay on the floor throughout [the rehearsal with Ronald Biggs] making no end of alterations and improvements, now there were going to be 2 players, and copying out yet another score for brother Tommy, all against time. Meanwhile Jimmy and Ronald were going through the rehearsal – rolls on all the drums – glockenspiels, marimbas, rumbas being played, etc. At 1 I finished. Both brothers jumped at me and we rehearsed hard till 1.50 then I got a cup of coffee and a filthy sandwich and tore by taxi to Charing Cross Road to the recording studios arriving 20 minutes later. Set straight to work on the film with Director to chalk in the cues . . .

This went on until 3.15 when the Blades brothers arrived. The strain of recording was terrible for me though I feel more at ease now. As there were two players I had to conduct and I am not an experienced conductor. I had to watch the screen to keep the pace of the music and follow cues; the commentator was on my left, drummers on my right, my score in front of me and a red light switch hung round my neck to signal to the recording chamber. I had to listen to the commentator and drop the music when he was speaking and give all cues to the drummers for synchronization watching the screen and my score and remembering to signal to some room for the synchronizing of a record for parts of the film. We worked till 6.30 without a break but the Blades brothers were not satisfied with one recording so we arranged for 8.30 a.m. on Wednesday; I was so exhausted I could scarcely speak! . . .

Thursday was more than dead and so restless. Did a hundred odd things and shopping in the morning. Lunched with Johnny Craxton and Lucian Freud – they were filthy from their studio work but very lively and stimulating. Johnny had done a lot of pictures since J's summer exhibition. Lucian having one at the Leicester later this autumn. Then went to look at show at the Redfern which I didn't like much. Went into Lefevre to see more but liked it less except for a vivid picture by Ethel Walker. But had a very interesting talk with Duncan McDonald the Director of the gallery who is not long back from New York. He is the greatest authority on the Impressionists in this country and its long since I saw him – first winter of the War when I lunched with him and his wife. It was good to talk about painting again. Then tried to get shoes ordered last Monday but still not my size! I'm walking on the pavement now – huge hole. Terribly short of coupons so can't get a coat. Haven't had one since 2 years before the War. In awful state of shabbiness . . .

33. Priaulx.

Today shopped for the weekend then went with David Gascoyne to Boosey and Hawkes Wigmore Concert. Heard a beautiful cantata by Britten "Rejoice in the Lamb". His simplicity and imagination is miraculous! It is music out of which one gets the utmost pleasure coming away with a feeling of joy and uplift, to use a vile word. We had tea together at a restaurant . . . David was in a wonderful mood of witticisms making nonsense rhymes and inverting the proverbs! You can't imagine how absurd they sound! He is such a sweet person apart from having a great mind and the most charming company. Then I got my bike out of pawn at Marylebone Station where it had reposed since last Sunday because I lost the ticket. We had a doodlebug or two these last nights – one new bang. I must now bath and go to bed.
Very much love and thanks for the bits,

Priaulx

CORNWALL AND LONDON

Images of Cornwall

Ever present, the wild, dark clamouring sea
The moorlands in primal remoteness with
  their stone circles and standing stones
The great winds, spray flying over
  the land
The linear rhythms of the hills,
  a counterpoint
  against the wild rhythms of the sea
Stones – sea – wind – light
One is renewed in relation to nature
  and the earth
One's ears listen in depth once more

P.R.

IN 1945 THE WAR ENDED. Priaulx was at work on a piece for strings which Michael Tippett had commissioned for the concerts at Morley Hall. It was at this time that she met Barbara Hepworth and Ben Nicholson, and was invited to stay with them in Cornwall, in St. Ives, where they had lived since the outbreak of war. This was the start of a friendship which was to influence both her life and work.

In London, where she lived at 75 Ladbroke Grove, Kensington, Priaulx was absorbed in composing, attending concerts and plays, and visiting galleries. She was in daily contact with musicians and artists, and when she stopped work for the day would often gather with friends for conversation. She was interested in almost everything, except the mundane and trivial, and enjoyed discourse on Galileo, space, the stars and planets; Picasso, abstraction in art; books ranging from Darwin to T.S. Eliot and Rilke, and always, of course, music. She was appointed Chamber Music coach at William Glock's Summer School of Music (first at Bryanston, then at Dartington) where she enjoyed weeks devoted entirely to music. International

34. Ben Nicholson in his St. Ives studio, 1953.

35. With Anne Glock.

36. William Glock at the summer school.

37. With Elliott Carter in Barbara Hepworth's garden.

figures gathered at the School to coach and perform, to attend classes, or simply to listen – lovers of music whoever they were. These summer schools, where she was able to exercise her great gifts as a teacher, brought a sense of release after the years of war and the urge to compose again.

Tippett's commission resulted in *Sinfonia da Camera* for string orchestra which was performed in London, then Paris, Geneva and Munich. Her String Quartet was performed at the Edinburgh Festival, and she was offered a commission from the South African Broadcasting Corporation for a trio suite.

Priaulx decided to move to St. Ives, and rented a small studio, Alison's Studio, almost on eye level with the sea in the old part of the town known as Downalong. The pattern her life was to follow henceforth became established. She divided her time between London – for the professional activities necessary to keep her up to date with all that was going on in music, particularly contemporary music – and Cornwall – where she came to compose, working alongside two of the most creative minds in the country. Barbara Hepworth and Ben Nicholson were becoming a central force in her life in St. Ives; in London Michael Tippett and William Glock were among her loved and trusted friends. She invited people to her flat, and was in turn invited, once to a Christmas dinner given by Edith Sitwell. The poet Stephen Spender was there; so was Michael Tippett. It was not only the conversation that held her fascinated, but also Edith Sitwell's commanding presence: later she was to set one of her poems to music.

38. The Amadeus Quartet.

39. Igor Stravinsky (*left*) with Elliott Carter, 1962.

It was at this time, in the late 1940s, that Priaulx wrote *Dance of the Rain.* The words were taken from a text by Eugene Marais, translated by the poet Uys Krige. She had collected many of Krige's poems, always with the idea that one day she might see the way to set them to music. *Dance of the Rain* was written to be performed by tenor or soprano, and guitar, as was *Ubunzima* (Misfortune) which followed it. The words were taken from a Zulu text, the first lines of which read:

> Misfortune has befallen the Land.
> Dark clouds hang over the earth . . .

These two songs were followed immediately by the *Barbaric Dance Suite* for piano. William Glock, writing of the influences of Priaulx's early environment on her music at this time, says:

> This may be seen . . . in its rhythms, its melodic outlines, its constant evocation of the sound of drums, and in its preoccupation with the tritone which probably came from hearing the native reed-flute ensembles whose scales were often characterised by that interval.

Priaulx was beginning to receive critical acclaim, and was offered more commissions. The Amadeus Quartet made a recording of her String Quartet for Decca. Then, to her intense delight, she met Igor Stravinsky at a dinner in London. Stravinsky was one of the most powerful and inspiring influences in her life as a composer, and she felt privileged to meet him. On this, the first occasion, he was captivated because she remembered some of the difficult click sounds in the Zulu language, and demonstrated them to him: between courses he attempted to imitate them. She met him again at Glock's Summer School and, after morning rehearsals of his work, had the daily pleasure of taking him back to his house, some ten minutes distance. He talked to her of many things, and wished he could live in England, because he said, 'It is the only country where one can be anonymous.' He also spoke to her of Turner's water-colours which he greatly admired.

Although the war was over it had left a legacy of mutilated bodies and broken minds. Among the casualties was Priaulx's sister Yollande. Fluent in several languages, she had been working in Vienna and was trapped there by the war. She became increasingly disturbed by all she saw and, because she could speak to the victims, understood too well their despair. Her breakdown was progressive and eventually permanent. Priaulx, who had been caring for her, doing everything she could to help, had finally to accept the opinions of the doctors. Yollande was placed in psychiatric care, never to come out except for holidays with Priaulx, or Nella when she came over from Cape Town. Every Sunday until Yollande's death (two years before her own) Priaulx made special sandwiches with the fillings her sister liked best, packed up raisins, nuts and candied peel, and a piece of fruit cake if she had any and, taking the package with her, visited her sister; faithfully, whether there was response or not, for over thirty years. When she was in St. Ives, her friends went. She wrote once a week, and if she was going to be out of England for a long period she prepared a stack of postcards – of Greece, Italy, Africa – places her sister had been to and liked, writing with forethought of the autumn and leaves falling, which they were not when she was departing but would begin to do before she returned. Friends would be charged to post them in successive weeks.

40. Benjamin Britten and Peter Pears, 1967.

1950 saw the completion of the Ballet Suite for Orchestra, which was followed by a commission from Benjamin Britten and Peter Pears. In her search for a suitable text Priaulx was helped by Elizabeth Sprigge, translator and biographer. She finally chose to set the text from John Donne's *Devotions.* The work which resulted was *Cycle for Declamation.* Peter Pears was to sing it and, influenced by the perfection of his diction, she decided to write it as an unaccompanied piece for tenor, or solo soprano, making exactly timed silences between the sentences to allow each thought to penetrate and another to arise. Always interested in silence, *listening* to silence, calculating silences between words and notes, her eye was further extended by Barbara Hepworth's conversations on spatial forms and Ben Nicholson's on linear movements and colour.

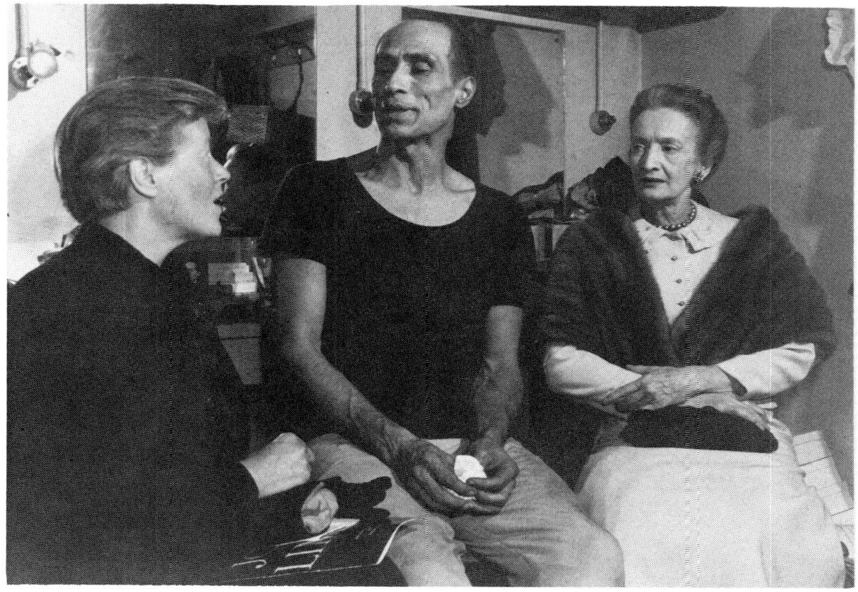

41. With José Limón and Doris Humphrey after a performance of *Night Spell.*

Suddenly and tragically Priaulx's adored brother Peter, with whom she always kept in touch – his life as vigorous and exciting as her own, died in a hotel fire. Thousands of miles away, she received a matter-of-fact report of his death with not enough knowledge to help the grieving. Nella, also heart-broken writing every week from South Africa, now became more eager for news of Priaulx's musical activities; the dramas as well as the triumphs. According to Priaulx's definition, dramas minor and major frequently beset the rehearsing of a piece, or the players, or its performance – or all three.

Drama can also be splendid. One such occasion came now, for the José Limón Dance Company of New York requested permission to use the String Quartet for a ballet which they called *Night Spell.* The dance again! The dancers she pronounced 'superbly imaginative'. They performed the ballet at Sadler's Wells Theatre and made a film of it, afterwards giving performances in America. It was choreographed by Doris Humphrey.

In 1953 Priaulx was elected a Fellow of the Royal College of Music, and was awarded the Collard Fellowship for Composition by The Worshipful Company of Musicians. Barbara Hepworth, about to embark on her first film, *Figures in a Landscape,* asked her to write the music for it – a very different prospect from the percussive music for *Fire in Our Factory.*

42. Priaulx's view of The Island from her piano.

Then, Priaulx, Barbara Hepworth and Michael Tippett conceived the idea of a festival in St. Ives for Coronation Year – its aim to commemorate the two Elizabethan ages in music, drama and the visual arts. It brought together local choirs and soloists from far afield – among them the counter-tenor Alfred Deller. It offered recitals, the plays of Shakespeare, a fanfare from the church tower composed by Tippett, and a very fine concert with *Rejoice in the Lord* conducted by Michael Tippett, with the Redruth Choir. It was a week of music which took months to organize. The Bishop of Truro, an active supporter of the Festival, was delighted when Priaulx sent him a kiss at the end of a telegram. She had not. The Post Office had misinterpreted the 'x' at the end of her name.

Priaulx now purchased a small studio in St. Ives, tucked against Tregenna Steps, almost under them. The Steps run down steeply through the town to the harbour. The studio was secluded and had a unique view out across The Island and Coastguard house to the horizon. Very quickly she made it her own, opening up part of the wall beside the big window in the main studio, and putting in glass. Direct lighting from two huge skylights helped counteract the drab dark grey walls. She set to work with friends to paint the inside white, and gave herself more light with an arrangement of squares and rectangles of mirrors set above the window-frame to catch the sun from the skylights above and reflect it back into the studio – an idea she had seen in studios in Paris.

43. Inside the St. Ives studio.

44. The entrance, with honey suckle, vine and bamboos.

Priaulx established a garden in a very small space, making a fascinating arrangement of unusual shrubs and other plants – wild if she could get them. Between the stones she planted exquisite small flowers – snowdrops, primroses, crocuses and alpine cyclamen. She even found space for a lawn. While she was building the garden she often sought the advice of Viscount Chaplin. The Chaplins lived close to Dartington and had become friends of Priaulx's because of their love of music. They admired her work and often invited her to their house, where they would discuss music and botany, listen to Anthony play, and wander through the garden with its many rare plants. Priaulx's own garden lawn was no bigger than a small room, but she took her guests there if it was fine. Visitors came from St. Ives, London, and abroad. They arrived at the secluding black garden door and their presence was anounced by a Georgian carriage bell which she had fitted to the inside of the door, its spring giving the bell a particularly clear tone.

45. The Obermeier; line of starling scarer visible on the wall.

Many famous people knew the sheltered garden with its aromatic scents, minute flowers, and the cries of gulls, and were invited to observe Priaulx's wildlife in the form of birds. Much as she loved cats, and they her, she would not have one at the studio because of her birds. She built a small bird-table in the middle of the lawn and, once she had become aware of the devastating effects of the starlings' gluttony on the food resources of the table, she constructed a starling scarer. Inside the studio was a square frame, to which she attached a fishing line which ran up the wall from where she sat at the piano, through a hole above the window-frame, and out across the small patio in a straight line to the bird-table. That end of the line was tied to a long bamboo which stood upright against one of the outriders of the bird-table. As she sat composing at the piano, or working on scores at a small table by the window, she had merely to pull the cord when the starlings descended to cause the bamboo to leap in the air, scattering the starlings. The bamboo fell back unerringly on to the outrider. The starlings hated it, but the other birds came to know that it was protecting their larder, and were often to be seen riding on it. Priaulx also made a barometer that worked accurately, and visitors seeing it were reminded of her seafaring ancestors.

Many of the shrubs and flowers in the garden were chosen to provide food for the birds and nectar for bees and butterflies. Priaulx began a book of Nature Notes – alas, with spasmodic entries as the demands of her musical life in London often called her away. But she was always in St. Ives over Christmas with Nella. Like her diaries and letters, her Nature Notes were details of the seasons, winds and tides, as well as the intimate life of her garden:

> *[1964] Christmas Tide Tregenna Steps Studio, St. Ives*
> Wildest gales. Sleet, hail, raging winds, very cold. After Christmas Day of frost walked up to Knills and in lanes behind with Nella. Brilliant and hot sun clearer sky than usual. Field full of field fares searching for worms, standing erect. Stripe from eye very noticable. Snowdrops in bloom end of December; bitterly cold winds.
>
> *[January 1965]* Sunday. One of the worst N.W. gales remembered: three waves engulfed the Lifeguard Station 60 feet above sea level, breaking thick glass, shooting high above the horizon line from this altitude. Continuous violent squalls all this January; the worst I remember.
>
> *[Later in January]* At last easing up of continuous squalls of hail and rain. *Birds* violently active on table and tits at nuts, fat, coconut. Robin brought female – very flighty. He withdrew from the table allowing her to feed – after weeks of chasing solitary female Black Cap and tits off "his" food. All birds have begun to flit and peck and chase. Great commotion in garden. Sometimes 10 tits at once on the frame. The family of 7 blue tits reared here last summer are in constant evidence. Also the smallest coal tit ever observed – they are the cheekiest of all. *Flowers* still bloom; Kaffir lilies since last September; Blue African daisies; Phlomis still blooming and with buds. Rosemary forming buds. Wallflowers breaking into bloom. A pink, large leafy plant in full bloom.
>
> *[23 January]* 8 a.m. Robin being really vicious. Driving everyone off the table by dive bombing – especially the Black cap female. A second Black cap female came today for the first time, very timid, slender and beautiful. Tremendous animation all flying back and forth tits, etc., at great speed. A mild morning after gentle rain all night. No wind. Promise of a better day.
>
> *[24 January]* 8.30 a.m. Birds excessively active. First buds on Polyanthus, 3 Pinks out. In the Studio sun down to the first bar of the frame – it was the first quiet night for many weeks.
>
> *[1 February]* First sun on bird table. Yellow Crocus open. Bitter E.S.E. wind. Barometer high.

46. At work in London at the Steinway.

From the studio Priaulx could look out over the North Atlantic and listen for the 'dark' tones of the sea. At the Cape it had been the South Atlantic. She had a one-third share in a boat, with Barbara Hepworth, and the historian Frank Halliday who lived in St. Ives. The critic Herbert Read was in it one day, with Frank at the oars. The gulls were excited by their approach and flung themselves into the air crying: Herbert drew attention to the fact that they were producing a word, calling her name, 'Priaulx, Priaulx, Priaulx'.

She worked in two sessions – the first in the morning – at a Steinway Grand in London, or an Obermeier Upright in St. Ives. Her manuscript, with work from the previous evening, would be on the music stand; and her pencils, sharpener and rubber on the bass end of the keyboard, the pencils very black and soft, yet able to be sharpened to needlepoint without breaking. Barbara Hepworth suggested the brand to suit her and she continued to use it throughout her life.

47. Barbara Hepworth, photographed by Priaulx.

48, 49. Barbara Hepworth's sculptures in progress, photographed by Priaulx.

She would work with great concentration until one o'clock, when she would lunch and then go out walking – in London in the park behind the houses in Ladbroke Grove, visiting friends, or going in to Elizabeth Sprigge, who owned the house at 75 Ladbroke Grove, if she was free, often tending the garden on Elizabeth's terrace. In St. Ives she would visit Barbara Hepworth, Ben Nicholson or the potter Bernard Leach (who had lived in St. Ives since 1920), gather a few wild flowers or berries to take home and put in a vase, climb up to Knills Steeple (a monument above the town) or walk along the cliffs with Frank Halliday before returning to the second session which she liked to begin at five o'clock, working until eight, sometimes nine if she was at the end of a piece. The routine was not unrelenting, but was followed when she was meeting a deadline. She attended concerts – not opera – art exhibitions, and the theatre. There was also the professional side of her life to attend to – the endless letters, publishers to be seen, rehearsals and interviews. She had no secretary, but those who had studied under her would always help when they could.

Priaulx was frequently asked by Ben Nicholson to come and look at a painting in progress, and was fascinated to become aware of something that did not happen in music – a spatial relationship, the linking of lines from the wonderful lines of hills in Cornwall, which she remarked upon often: lines that were apart from the form of the land and the sea. These spatial relationships which she saw daily in the work of Barbara Hepworth and Ben Nicholson made her aware of the importance of line, and of juxtapositions and textures, and she felt they had an effect on her writing. She was never able to say precisely how this affected her music, only that it did.

Ben Nicholson gave her many drawings and small paintings, photographs and reproductions of his work, and some large originals. The most treasured of these was an oil painting of Tula, his Siamese cat. They had watched together as Tula rushed up and down trees and around the garden, following the flick of her black tail and the occasional glimpse of blue eyes. Priaulx thought that the black lines in the painting had something to do with the flicking tail of the skittish Tula, and the fine, sharp shape of blue with her eyes. The painting hung beside her bed in London, the last thing she saw before sleeping.

Ben and Barbara had introduced her to Bernard Leach, and to her delight he offered her his wheel, gave her a wodge of clay and instructed her how to throw it. Taking it from the kiln after firing, they both wondered what it was she had tried to shape, and burst into laughter, turning her failure into closer friendship. He invited her to comment on his pots because her first remarks always concerned their resonance. She enjoyed any conversation he cared to offer her because of his wisdom, the East-West manner in which he looked at things, his unfaltering choice of good English, and *his* search for the truth. Both appreciated fine food, different food, new experiences. He would offer her a flat, dark green square of Japanese seaweed, which she would savour as he watched intently, awaiting her opinion, always honest and precise. She invited him to the studio, having prepared a special hors-d'oeuvre or soup, delighting in his immediate reaction to the smell, sniffing the air as he came in the door, anticipating he knew not what – loving it, loving her.

50. Ben Nicholson with cat.

51. Ben Nicholson's painting of Tula.

52. Bernard Leach,1968.

53. (*Overleaf*) From the score of *Quanta*. (*Reproduced by kind permission of Schott & Co. Ltd.*)

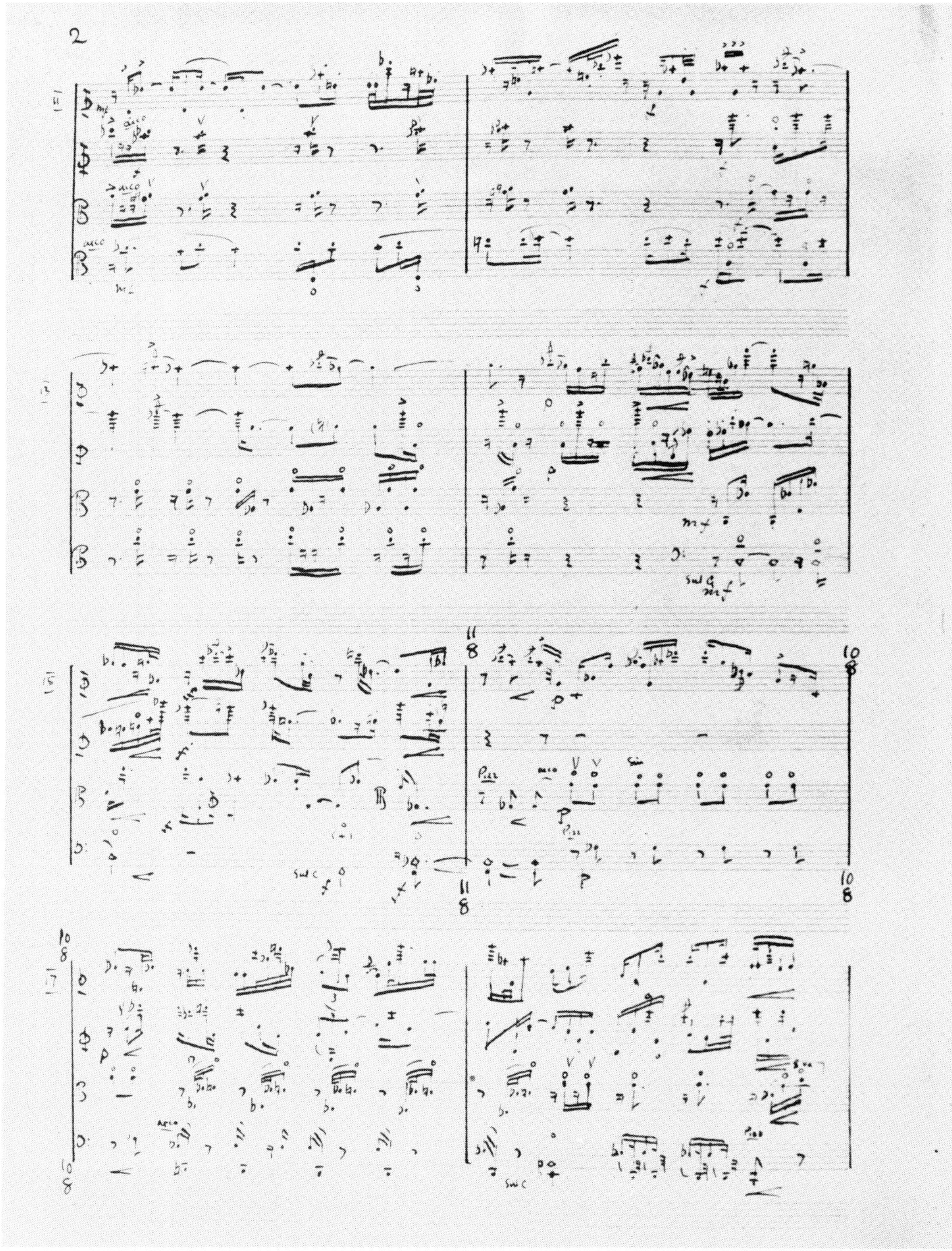

3.
pp

Priaulx's reputation was growing. There was the first performance of Six Pieces for Five Wind Instruments, written in 1957, and the following year, while at work on the *Pastoral Triptych* for solo oboe, she was commissioned by the London Philharmonic Society to write the opening piece for a concert in honour of Adrian Boult's ten years with the Orchestra. Very excited by this she wrote the Dance Concerto 'Phala-Phala' for full orchestra, including a 'concourse of horns'. During one section Boult was heard to shout over the thundering of the orchestra, 'No music for an old fogie like me.'

With Elizabeth Sprigge in London, working in the flat below her on translations of Strindberg and her biography of Gertrude Stein – always something in progress –and Barbara and Ben in St. Ives, dedicated to their work, she had in both places what she called strong currents of inspiration. In an interview for *Ideas of Today* she said:

> Ben Nicholson once said to me that one must work every day because it takes so long to reach the level where ideas begin to flow. You have to get yourself into some psychological state in order to reach the level where original ideas rise, though you yourself may not be fully conscious of what is taking place. Beethoven said, on hearing an earlier work of his after a long period had passed, that when he wrote it he had no idea of the content – there was much more in it than he had conceived of at the time. It is as if one has to hold oneself on a level where ideas are free to flow out rather than being intellectually forced out. After the free flow, an artist works at it with all his craft. One must exercise control over excitement in order to preserve the critical faculty, which is so important.

With a commission from the BBC for the newly-established Invitation Concerts she began work on *Quanta*. Always interested in the universe and universals, in space, the stars and planets, she would read and re-read the writings of Johannes Kepler, underlining passages which struck her:

> If observed from the sun the proportion between the wave-lengths of certain planets is the same as the relation between the lengths of chords producing harmonic tones.

> Pythagoras, who believed that the majesty of philosophy is present in *nothing but silence.*

54. The London Oboe Quartet. (*L. to r.*) Perry Hart, Brian Hawkins, Kenneth Heath and Janet Craxton.

55. As Circus Whip, with Barbara Hepworth.

With these thoughts and impressions operating subconsciously in her mind, the work was destined to be of outstanding significance. Timothy Baxter, writing in *The Composer* states:

> *Quanta* proved to be a key work; a chamber work for oboe and string trio. There is a link between its title and the Quantum theory of energy existing in space, independent of matter, though the word *Quanta* did not come into the composer's mind until the work was nearing its completion. The concept of energy particles gradually congregating and joining together, only to burst out again violently has a parallel in the music where tight clusters of sound are gradually built up then broken into fragments.
>
> The unusual nature of this work, its taut 12 minute argument and brittle rhythmic patterns, make it most arresting, and Priaulx Rainier herself feels that, with *Quanta*, she had reached a new level of writing.

Quanta was played frequently by the London Oboe Quartet, and taken into their repertoire.

Gradually, the town of St. Ives gave Priaulx a sense of belonging. Her studio provided the solitude in which to create; Barbara and Ben, the Hallidays and Bernard Leach, the close and admiring support she needed; and the fun. The Arts Ball was always an occasion in the year when they would take a rest from work, combine their talents, often make their fancy dress costumes and proceed in spectacular and grand style to the Ball, everyone playing whatever man, woman or beast they represented. One year Priaulx was the Circus Whip. Before the ball she had gone down to a cove hidden by rocks to practise cracking her whip. On the night of the Ball she waited until the spirit of the occasion was well advanced. Suddenly, in the midst of the din and buzz, there was an explosive crack at very close quarters. People jumped as if a gun had gone off. There was total silence, then laughter as the culprit was located – smiling, eyes alight, slightly astonished at what the rehearsals in the cove had produced.

Priaulx's music astonished audiences and critics alike, and there was something else about her that did too:

> Two elderly clergymen were seated in a box at the Proms in 1964. Moments before the first performance of Priaulx Rainier's *Cello Concerto* one said to the other: 'What do you think we are in for now?' 'Let me see now' said the other. 'Born 1903 – Oh, I think we'll be alright, don't you?' After the performance of this unusual and disturbing work they sat for a moment in stunned silence until one spied the composer coming down the steps to take a bow. He said to the other in complete astonishment: 'It's a woman!'
>
> Perhaps it is hardly surprising that they should have reacted in this way since the music of Priaulx Rainier has a robust and commanding manner, highly charged with dissonance and jolting, fragmented rhythms with constantly changing textures. Without recognisable thematic material, it is not always easy to get to grips with at one hearing, though the outstanding quality of the work does make an immediate impression. One wonders how much audiences concern themselves with the fact that a work is not only new but also by a female composer, rather than with the actual music itself. (Timothy Baxter writing in *The Composer*.)

56. Jaqueline du Pré, 1969.

The Cello Concerto was dedicated to Jacqueline du Pré, who first performed it, playing, Priaulx said, 'most eloquently'. A long note held by the cello led into the second movement, and sounds fading away in harmony from the cello ended it. It had been preceded by the Suite for Solo Cello and Viola and was followed by her String Trio which consisted of two parts. The dominance of the cello in these works did not mean any repetition of structures, tone, texture or phrasing – Priaulx was incapable of repeating herself or deriving ideas from a completed work as the germ of another, different merely in form. Others did it, and she did not criticise them. She felt they were fortunate to be able to work from something already created, but the fact remained that for her such a work did not have its own source, and was therefore derivative. She applied the same standards to painting and sculpture, indeed to all forms of creativity; for her there *was* something new under the sun. The years with Hepworth, Nicholson and Leach had refined and extended her response to all art forms and her relationship to her own. She saw work by others

57. Scoring.

58. Found in an envelope marked 'Special Friends'.

derived from that of Hepworth, Nicholson and Leach and, while recognizing this as a necessary extension of any creative artist's mind, leading inevitably towards the next revolution in the arts, she could not do it.

The BBC was preparing a programme for Michael Tippett's fiftieth birthday, and asked Priaulx to give a half-hour talk about his life and work. Soon after she was given an Invitation Concert for her own works, including two first performances. At the same time she was working on a large orchestral piece, also commissioned by the BBC, for the 1967 Cheltenham Festival. An ambitious work for divided orchestra, representing the light and dark sides of the moon, it was called *Aequora Lunae* (Seas of the Moon), the movements representing seas of ice, water, thunder, rain, clouds . . . her fascination with space and love of nature; her poetic Images of the Moon. She was not overjoyed when man reached it, trod on it, and stuck 'a little tin flag' in it. She always read the reviews of her work, and where there was criticism she heeded it, looked at the piece again, considered it carefully and often made alterations. The reviews of *Aequora Lunae* were mixed, but one delighted critic, heading his review 'The Rainier Flair and Bite', suggested that it was best to ignore the written score in order to 'lay back your lugs and listen' . . . she concurred.

A friend had given Priaulx a beautifully knitted Zulu mask which stretched to cover her head completely and could be pulled on and off in a second. It was red; its top-knot black, its eyes, mouth and nostrils ringed with black and white, green slashes crossing the head and decorating the cheeks. It could be carried very easily in her handbag or even in a pocket, and she was given to taking it secretly to the dining-table on festive occasions, saying nothing, biding her time. If an appropriate moment did not present itself the mask remained concealed. But if the food and wine, the occasion and conviviality were all as she wished, with superb timing and extreme deftness, she would bend as if to retrieve her fallen table napkin, sit up and utter a few blood-curdling words of Zulu right into the ear of the person next to her, who would turn in amazement at the attack and remain stunned by the apparition she presented. Any guests present who were unaware of this side of her were left speechless. The expressive, gesturing hands would be spread, palms upmost, as her eyes through their black and white surrounds slowly circled the table. Then, with one swift movement, the mask was off, never to be donned again on that occasion.

The entire act was over in one or two minutes, but its effect was imprinted vividly for days, if not forever, in the minds of the beholders. How she enjoyed 'acting up', as she called it. It was done with such naturalness and lack of exhibitionism that she would have the whole place in an uproar, the dinner guests in a state of full-bodied laughter, herself included, until she closed her eyes to shut out the mischief and bowed her head slightly in a small smile of genuine pleasure at her success. She was never certain what the result would be, but was willing to take risks, just as she had done when she wrote her first Quartet in 5/8 time, or sailed single-handed around the Cornish coast in a boat that had belonged to Sir Arthur Quiller-Couch.

Priaulx loved evenings of riotous fun, to which she was ever ready to contribute with her laughter and her anecdotes. If Mozart's name was mentioned, knowing that in his letters he frequently referred to a certain percussive sound from the body, and using him as an authority for good taste, she would embark on her own anecdotal theme and variations of it. For all her riotousness, her fun was perfectly perceived with never a misjudged act or word. After an evening such as this, despite the hour, if it was fine she would stand quite still in the night, straighten her shoulders, her hands laced behind her back, her face towards the sky – listening to the stars singing.

TRAVELS

PRIAULX LOVED TRAVELLING. It offered a release from the pressures of composing, from the compulsion that drove her to it; it refreshed her physically and mentally. Driving through the heart of the French countryside she would open her arms to embrace nature: 'What's to hinder?' she would cry from the crest of a hill, a long straight road in front of her. Up before the stars disappeared, bathing in mountain streams, lakes or the sea, she climbed and rambled, often trekking for miles. Although her driving was, as Michael Tippett states, 'incomparably erratic' she never had a serious accident. Tippett also speaks of her 'celebrated vagueness about arrangements and directions'; on one occasion she directed him to the place where she was staying, saying, 'Take the second exit on the roundabout before the last one.'

Although she went to Tenerife and the United States, and revisited South Africa, it was Europe that drew her. After the first grand tour with Miss Horniman, she often travelled to France with Elizabeth Sprigge – one of the most memorable visits was during Elizabeth's research for her biography of Gertrude Stein.

In the 1960s Nella retired from her post as music teacher at the University College and joined Priaulx in England, taking an upper floor flat in the same house. Their lives never in conflict, both loving the same music, Nella knowledgeable and supportive – always the protector as she had been in Africa, reading under the great tree, or practising at the piano – both enjoyed the same life, although they were very different. Now there was someone else to visit Yollande, and more constant contact with their brother's son, Peter, who had lived with Nella throughout his teens and been educated by her. Married and working in the oil industry he lived in many countries – Canada, Australia, North and South America – and travelled to many more. His two sisters were in Africa, and Priaulx wrote to them; her letters, as they always had done, holding the family together and proof of her deep affection for them.

59. Ready to leave.

60. Elizabeth Sprigge in France.

61. Nella climbing.

62. At Dino.

Priaulx and Nella were now able to travel together. They went most often to France, but their journeys took them to Norway and Finland, and as far east as Turkey. They carried everything in rucksacks; Nella was expert at making profitable use of every bit of space. Five feet tall, with bones as thin as a bird's and lovely, delicate features, her upright figure and gentle manner gave the appearance of someone precious, from another age. Men felt chivalrous in her presence. Yet she climbed the Drakensbergs, with rucksack, boots and slacks, sleeping in a pup tent or on the ground; went to Namibia; did a journey up the Nile; drove a van which the French named *Rapide*; and climbed Mount Olympus, undaunted and fearless.

Priaulx had favourite places which she visited again and again. Ménerbes in the south of France was one. She went frequently with Nella, met Michael Tippett there, made a water-colour of the town, and wrote of it to William Glock:

63. Priaulx's water-colour of Ménerbes.

> Suddenly among the foothills we saw Ménerbes – a medieval legendary town built 500 feet above the valley on a rocky crag – a pile of ruined castles and ancient buildings, for it's built on Greek and Roman remains. The rock is shaped like a ship. The tower (in which we're staying) is at the narrow end looking over both sides; up a narrow valley to the Luberon, and out over rolling cultivated land and pine forests to Mt. Ventoux, snow capped, 30 miles away. Like the monasteries of olden times, remote from the world, yet looking down from seclusion upon its activities. Below, the land has been formed by many men's loves throughout the centuries – a pattern of vineyards, olive groves, white roads winding past old turreted farmhouses, disappearing into the distant forests. Its medievalism is strong, clear cut and "sauvage" not soft and sentimental like the German fairy tale towns.

As Glock observed:

> That last sentence says much about her own artistic personality and beliefs, and the whole passage might almost belong to Goethe's *Italian Journey* for its deep knowledge of nature and of natural processes. All this affected her music, I'm sure, [as] did her insight into the works of Barbara Hepworth, Ben Nicholson and a few others whose imaginative ideals seem to correspond to her own.

64. Winifred Katzin in Switzerland.

Switzerland was another country she visited as much as she could. Ben Nicholson lived there now; so did Winifred Katzin (she had married), and Priaulx never missed an opportunity to see her and exchange ideas, or simply listen to the person she revered for her learning, intellect and judgement, and who 'has been in my life always.'

In the standards she upheld, her care and concern, the gentleness and magnanimity she showed toward those she knew and loved, there was not an iota of space for what she considered vulgar, common, or inconsequential. Anything she met that was destructive of man's progress in his comprehension of the universe and of himself – particularly in the shape of a person – she would not admit. She would pass by without a word. But they knew. Priaulx's vibrations could curl around corners.

Later Years

FOR PRIAULX 1970 began with an invitation to the Carnegie-Mellon University, Pittsburgh, USA, for performances of her work and to lecture. While there she spent some time with David Lewis, author, architect and art critic, whom she had befriended in St. Ives, knew well and admired, and whose sense of the absurd could match her own.

In England later that year she went to the Aldeburgh Festival, to the first performance of *The Bee Oracles*, a work for tenor solo, flute, oboe, violin, cello and harpsichord, commissioned by Peter Pears. The words were from a poem by Edith Sitwell, derived from an ancient Indian text, and involved her in a long and difficult affair over copyright. Without the help of Sir Arthur Bliss, who thought highly both of her and her work, it is doubtful if she could have untangled the situation. She was beset by it throughout the writing of the work, her composing hours wasted trying to resolve it. She worked until one and two o'clock in the morning, writing in new phrases, copying and correcting the score, fearful that it would never be done in time. It was finished, it was performed, it was praised – and she was never to forget her indebtedness to Sir Arthur. It was not the only time that he gave her assistance and advice.

Quinque for harpsichord came next, to be followed by the Organ *Gloriana* commissioned by Barry Smith of St. George's Cathedral, Cape Town. Never having written for the organ, and not knowing in detail its full range, she sought assistance and was taken to a church in London where a priest gave her a demonstration. She was delighted and set to work immediately. Several months later, having delivered the score to the organist Christopher Bowers-Broadbent, she went with him to a rehearsal, remarking quietly at the end that she was surprised by what she had written.

> *Gloriana* suggests a paean of praise, and the work certainly is exultant and powerful, exploring opposed tonalities in cluster formations. Tough and gritty, hard as granite, its three movements conjure from the instrument a vast range of sounds which make one listen to the instrument in an entirely new way. Its style is uncompromising and authoritative; blaring dissonances are contrasted with muted tones and there are sudden bursts of fury. After a slow middle movement, the toccata-like finale boils up to a splendidly exhilarating climax, ending almost inaudibly in the highest register. (Timothy Baxter)

65. With David Lewis, on a picnic in Pittsburgh.

66. Sir Arthur Bliss, 1965.

In 1972 Priaulx was staying at Ploërmel, in France, and was attracted by the sound of church bells in the early morning and the effect of the first light of the sun as it shafted through the stained-glass windows. The images and sounds gave her the idea for a piece which the BBC had commissioned. She called it *Ploërmel* for wind and percussion, and dedicated it to her great friends Sir William and Lady Glock. Timothy Baxter wrote:

> The percussion section always a special feature of a Rainier score – has prominent use of tubular bells, hand bells, antique cymbals and *sonagli* with high and low pitched gongs, xylophone and marimba. Of all these the use of the marimba has become a familiar feature of the [her] orchestral works, being a direct link with the sounds of the music of South Africa.

Ploërmel was first performed at the Promenade Concerts in 1973. Priaulx was seventy years old, and the BBC also arranged a seventieth birthday programme when her work was performed at the Three Choirs Festival, the Bath Festival, and at Aldeburgh.

That year she completed *Duo: Vision and Prayer* for tenor and piano, the text from a poem by Dylan Thomas. She conceived the form for this work too in France, by an isolated lake in the Morvan country around Vézelay. She had already decided to set the text, but not *how* to set it. She was drawn instinctively by words which equated with and extended her own thoughts on man's comprehension of the universe and himself, and were a plea for hope in the future. Hence her choice of *Vision and Prayer.* Each verse of the poem appeared on the printed page in the shape of a diamond. Priaulx was usually indifferent to shaped poetry, but somehow the diamonds, arranged point to point, fascinated her and placed a new meaning on it: words and shape, she felt, were interdependent, and it had been the poet's intention to have them so. Very early one morning, after a swim in the lake, she took the text of *Vision and Prayer* into the forest of the Morvan, the night fragrance of lily of the valley still drifting in the air. There she set the form of the piece, making fine pencil notes against the verses. The result was an impassioned musical declamation of what she described as 'the fury and torrent of words, the call upon the Deity which makes the poem at times ferocious and wildly dramatic. A very great poem.'

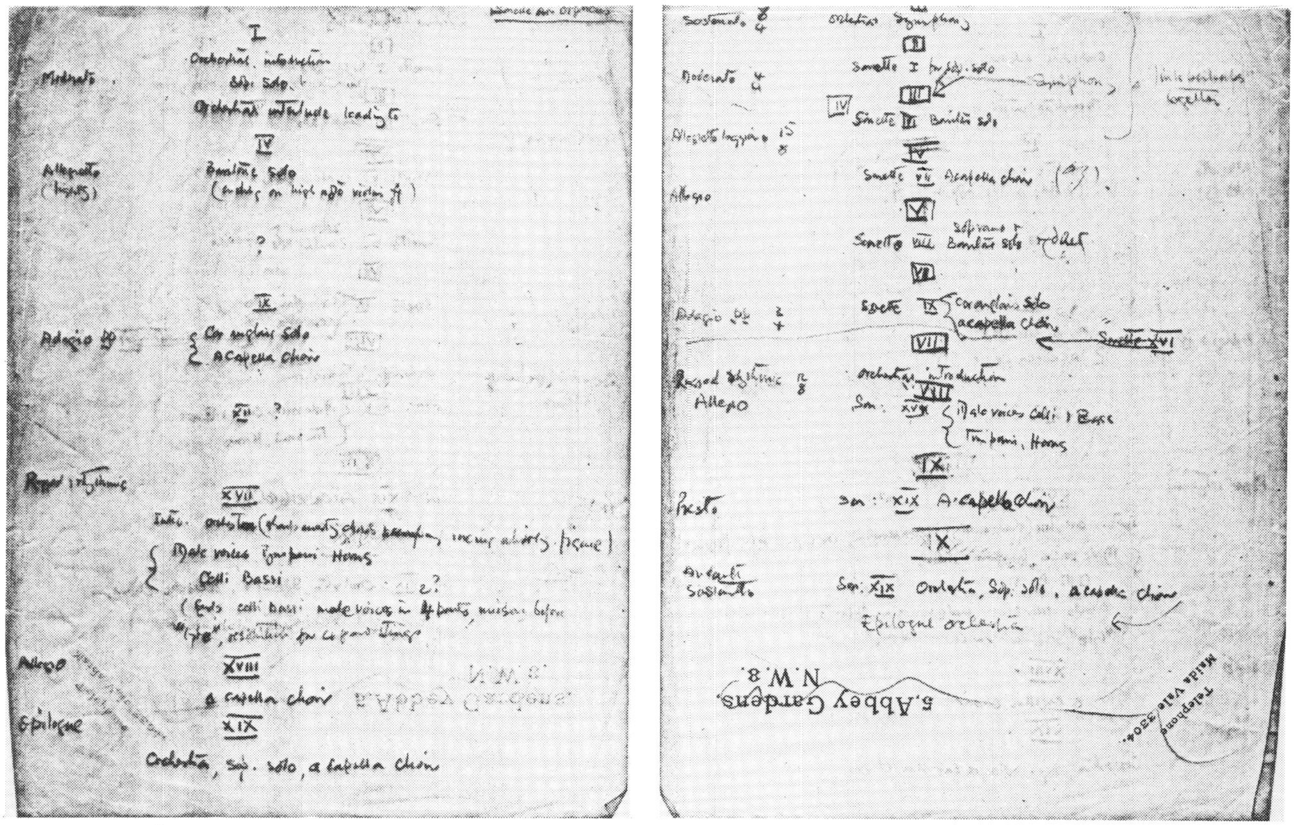

67. Notes on the *Sonnets.*

If Stravinsky was the composer Priaulx most admired, Rilke was the poet. She longed to set his words to music, particularly the *Sonnets to Orpheus*, and carried a hardback copy of them with her, to consider and reconsider. Inside, on two sheets of headed paper, were notes on how she had planned the structure of the work, and pencilled ideas on the choral section: 'Great Unison – voices, orchestra: orchestra, solo'. On the facing page, at the beginning of the *Sonnets*, she had written six quotations from *Johannes Kepler: Life and Letters*; a quotation from Brancusi; another from Valéry. The words of Brancusi were underlined:

Voir loin est une chose, y aller est une autre.

Rilke was like a spiritual force or fire that pursued her. She was never really happy with the translations, wanting words which could match the syllabic form of the original text. She did not want her music to destroy anything of Rilke's – only to offer him her gift.

In 1974, at the suggestion of Francis Routh, Priaulx was writing again for the organ, for a Redcliffe concert. She called the piece *Primordial Canticles*. The idea occurred to her at a friend's house as she listened to a recording of the poignant nocturnal calls of the loon, and other wildlife cries coming across great stretches of water in long-drawn-out syllables reminding her of the sounds of the Zulus. Then she began to think about a setting for the poem *Prayers from the Ark*, which calls upon God to help protect Noah and the animals who utter them directly and in separate pleas. The poem was written by Carmen Bernos de Gasztold, from a Benedictine abbey in France; her work was for tenor and harp, and occupied her over a long period.

Priaulx imposed on herself exacting standards, demanding that each note have its intention, altering it if it did not, or taking it out if she suddenly discovered that the piece was better without it. This kind of commitment did not permit her to work fast. Integrity guided what she was and did, and even when she was deeply hurt, or betrayed, nothing broke it. Faults and imperfections she certainly had, but her integrity was inviolable and affected not only the pace at which she worked, but the number of works she completed.

In 1975, while Priaulx was writing *Prayers from the Ark*, Barbara Hepworth died, suffering the same tragic fate as her brother Peter. Priaulx was devastated. She felt she owed Barbara so much, both as a creative artist and as a friend. Her memories of her were clear in every detail – as on the day they had reshaped Barbara's garden (which was heart-shaped with rose beds) deciding that it needed a straight line of turf to give it form and distance. They had chosen to do it on Christmas Day because there would be neither staff nor visitors in the garden then. Priaulx brought turf from a building site; they took out the roses, made the line straight, and began to make what is now part of the Barbara Hepworth Museum, where the standing sculptures are.

68. Working in the St. Ives studio.

69. Barbara Hepworth. *(Reproduced by kind permission of Peter Kinnear.)*

70. A gift from Barbara Hepworth: *Group of Three Magic Forms*, **silver 1973.**

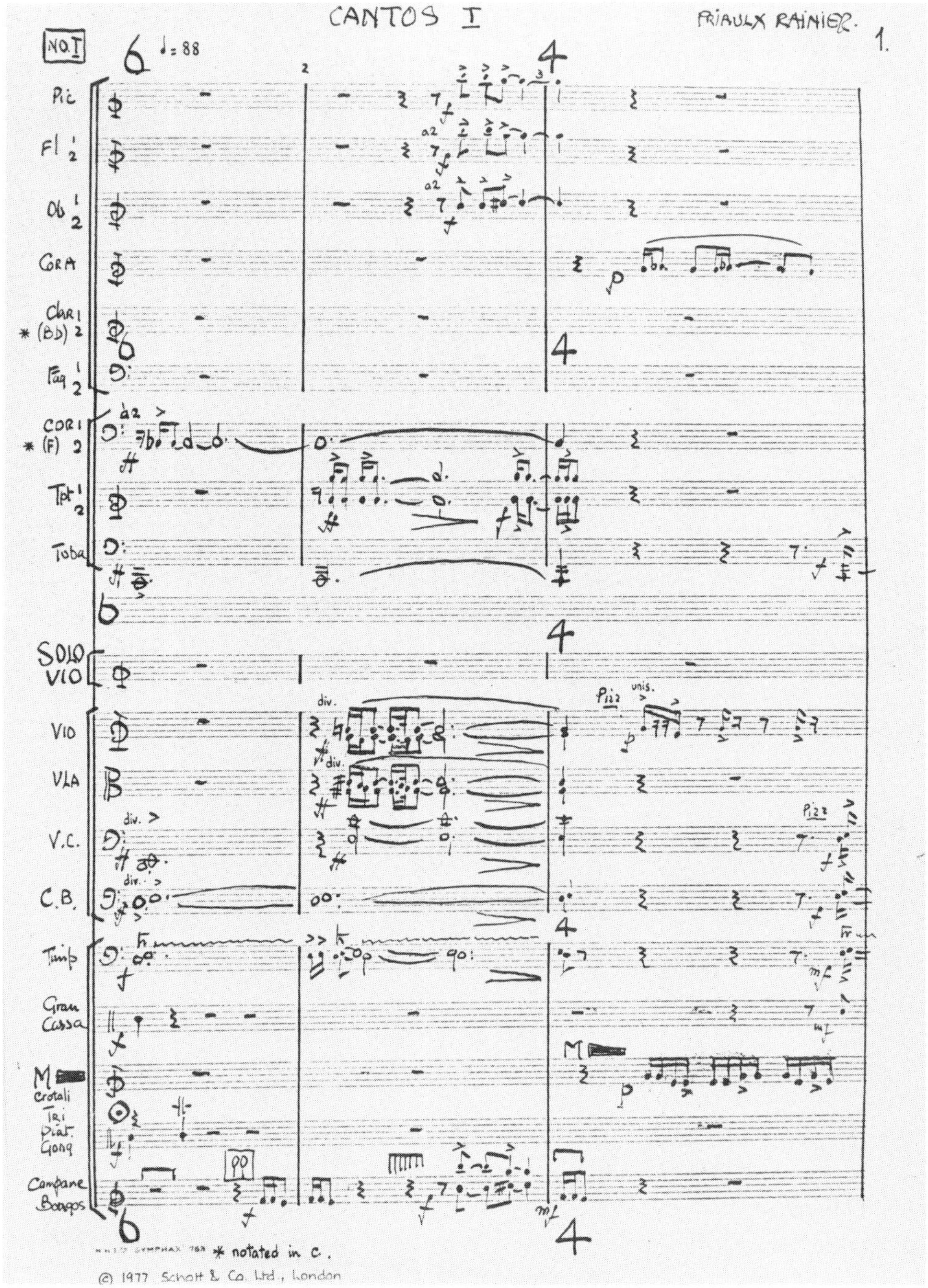

71. Score of *Due Canti.* (*Reproduced by kind permission of Schott & Co. Ltd.*)

72. Yehudi Menuhin.

Not long after Barbara's death Priaulx was asked by Yehudi Menuhin to write a violin concerto. She did not answer immediately; having been a violinist, she felt it would be difficult to invent fresh ideas for the instrument. However, she decided to accept, calling the piece *Due Canti e Finale* (Two Songs and Finale) because, as she explained, the violin is essentially a singing voice. The work also differed from a classical concerto in that there were no heavy orchestral sections, the orchestra taking part in a kind of dialogue with the solo violin. Menuhin wrote about the Concerto in the *Radio Times* comment:

> I owe Priaulx Rainier's delightful Concerto to my wife who read that this wonderful composer, though a former violinist, had never written a concerto for the instrument and suggested I should commission one. The result is a fascinating work, beautifully suited to the violin sound.

At a pre-concert talk Priaulx herself described the work as a dual between the solo violin, with its lyrical and decorative writing, and the orchestra, which is more

73 Rehearsing.

74. Janet Craxton.

fragmented and incisive. Although the title suggests a three-movement work, it is in fact in five movements – the three main ones are linked by a whimsical interlude and hushed recitative.

The BBC put on a series of six Sunday evening concerts of Priaulx's compositions, providing her with an opportunity to assess many years of work. In 1977 the Violin Concerto was given its first performance at the Edinburgh Festival, Menuhin playing, Sir Charles Groves conducting. It was played again by Menuhin at a Promenade Concert the following year. Priaulx's nephew Peter and his wife flew over from Canada to be present, and sat with Nella; ever-gracious, ever-loving Nella, a smile of pure joy lighting her face. Priaulx was called to the stage, and again there were murmurs of astonishment at her age and sex – which was left in no doubt when first Menuhin, then Sir Charles wrapped her in a fervent embrace, kissing her warmly, while Patricia Hughes broadcasting for Radio Three announced that the composer, who was racing down the stairs to take her call, was seventy-five years old.

75. Rehearsing *Requiem* with Peter Gellhorn (*centre*) and Philip Langridge.

That same year Priaulx was asked by Peter Norris to visit the Yehudi Menuhin School to coach students in a number of her works. She also began working on the *Duo Concertante* for two winds and orchestra which was dedicated to Janet Craxton. Janet and Thea King were to play the solo instruments. Ten days before the concert Janet died very suddenly. It was a shattering blow: it meant the loss to the musical world of a performer of outstanding musicianship; and to Priaulx of a personal friend – she had known Janet since she was two, and had also taught her. Also, of course, it left the *Concertante* without one of its principal soloists for whose eloquent playing Priaulx had devised special passages. The performance went ahead when Neil Black generously agreed to take over. It was received with the same tremendous enthusiasm as the Violin Concerto.

Great teacher that she was, the Menuhin School continued to invite Priaulx to come and coach. Every musician who knew her – composers, conductors, performers and those who were privileged to study under her – all speak of her amazing gift in interpreting music, and of her ability to impart this to them. She was always encouraging, never destroying, building up for them concepts of a work they had neither seen nor recognized within it.

76. Rehearsing *Requiem* at the Royal Albert Hall, August 1972.

Peter Gellhorn, who conducted *Requiem* at the Royal Albert Hall, with Philip Langridge, tenor, was introduced to Priaulx by Orrea Pernel who had asked her to listen to them rehearsing. He wrote of this occasion:

> She did indeed listen, and it seemed she heard everything, not only what was right or wrong, but why it was so. She judged the motive as well as the action; in the end one felt as if she knew all about you by hearing you play.
>
> . . . it was easy to submit to her criticism without any ill feeling, as it was given in a quiet, matter-of-fact manner without any personal accent, not so much an opinion as a reminder of what we knew to be true.

77. **David Gascoyne, who wrote the words for *Requiem*.**

78. **Nigel Butterley.**

The eminent Australian composer Nigel Butterley, who studied with Priaulx, wrote:

> Michael Tippett recommended Priaulx Rainier to me, describing her as the best teacher in his opinion in London. Certainly for me Priaulx was exactly right. She helped me to think and listen with a more enquiring mind, to be wary of what was obvious or predictable, to question what came easily. She expounded no special technique or theory, and rode no hobby-horse. As she wrote herself, some twenty years later, 'It was a moment in your work which was crucial and I happened to be the listening ear . . . this is how things come about.'
>
> She was a constant guiding force – most especially because of her absolute single-minded commitment to being a composer. There was no time for turning out pot boilers or insignificant trifles. One's work had to be of the highest quality and value, and therefore had the highest place in one's life. This was never stated in so many words, but is probably the most important thing I learned from her.

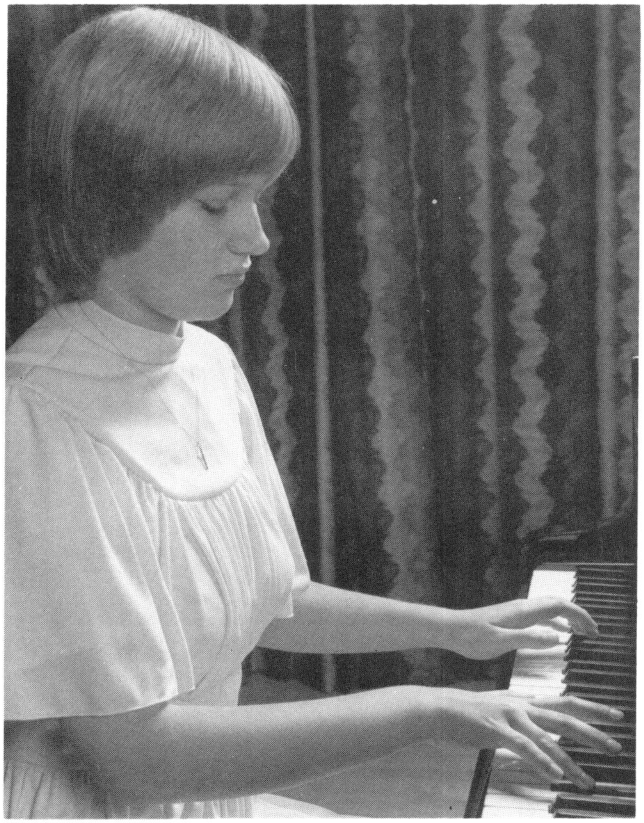

79. **Amanda Hurton, aged 16.**

80. Susie Mészáros.

81. Quartet from the Menuhin School. (*L. to r.*) Antonella Rallo, viola; David Smith, second violin; Robert Gibbs, first violin; Hannah Roberts, cello.

Continuing to be a 'listening ear' at the Menuhin School, Priaulx enjoyed coaching there, finding that the students encountered no difficulty in playing her work and responded to the challenge it offered. Two of them, Amanda Hurton, piano and Susie Mészáros, viola, gave several performances of her Sonata for Viola and Piano, one for French Radio. Four other students who had left the School were playing as a quartet and included Priaulx's String Quartet in their repertoire. She was continually invigorated by the close working relationships with students at the Menuhin School, all musicians of the future, representing hope to Priaulx whose life had been dedicated to making and creating music.

Then in 1979 her darling Nella died. She had moved to St. Ives and was living close to the studio. She had not been well so Priaulx, able to be with her every day, was not entirely unprepared. But nothing could replace such selfless and abiding love, and Priaulx, bereft, was now head of the family. At Nella's cremation the chapel was filled with her adored sister's music; her ashes were buried at Penmount, near Truro, on the crest of a high hill overlooking the contoured land of Cornwall, a space beside for Priaulx's.

An invitation to visit South Africa to undertake a lecture tour in no way deterred Priaulx. She toured the universities, lecturing and attending concerts of her work, giving introductory talks before each one. For many years she had corresponded with the author Mary Renault, and was delighted to visit her at the Cape. Despite the demands of the tour, she found time to be driven to her favourite places – Sea Point, Botany Bay and along the ridge which juts out into the sea at the southernmost tip of Cape Town.

82. Joan Dickson, cello, and Joyce Rathbone, a former student of Priaulx's.

83. Doctorate of Music (Honoris Causa), 1982.

When she returned to England she began work on the Grand Duo for Cello and Piano, played by Joan Dickson and Joyce Rathbone, first at the Wigmore Hall, then at the Bath Festival. It was to receive many public performances. Priaulx worked somewhat shorter hours now because she was diagnosed as having a mild form of angina. This frightened her, for it was what her father had reportedly died from, and she was concerned about her health until a pacemaker was fitted, giving her great mental relief.

In 1982 Priaulx was invited back to South Africa, this time to be honoured with a Doctorate of Music (Honoris Causa) by the University of Cape Town. Then it was her eightieth birthday. She received acclaim and messages of congratulation from all over the world, and in June of that year, replying to the Master's toast to the ladies at the Worshipful Company of Musicians, she said:

> The Master, Wardens, Assistants and Gentlemen, I am honoured to be asked to respond on behalf of the guests to your toast. It gives me particular pleasure for, though a guest at this dinner, I am also a Yeoman of the Company, having been awarded their Collard Fellowship for Composition. This came at a period of great need, enabling me to devote more time to my work.
>
> I was, I believe, the first female to receive this award – while being informed of the procedures the question of the livery arose, the Clerk of the Company remarking tentatively that I would perhaps be able to wear the Hood, but the question of the whole livery . . . and he hesitated – I helped him; 'Is it a question of the *Nether garments*?'
>
> The Worshipful Company with its long history of assistance to musicians, brings its activities up to date, helping young artists and, in many other ways, adding to our musical life. I feel its historic presence among us as something for which all musicians should be grateful, and we thank those who take on the cares of office and so continue for the future 'The Worshipful Company'.
>
> Once again we thank the Master, Wardens, Assistants and Gentlemen for their toast.

Soon after, in October, Priaulx was finally elected to the Livery. She had been admitted to the Freedom and become a Yeoman twenty years before, but it had not been the practice of a Worshipful Company to consider a female for the Livery. Slowly, however, the climate changed, and Priaulx became the first woman to be elected to the Livery of the Worshipful Company of Musicians since its formation in 1500.

In 1984 she was commissioned by the Jersey Wildlife Trust to write a piece for violin and orchestra. The director, Sir Gerald Durrell, had asked Yehudi Menuhin to recommend a composer to write a short orchestral work for their forthcoming twenty-fifth anniversary, to be performed by the Jersey Youth Orchestra with Menuhin as soloist and conductor. Menuhin recommended Priaulx because of her knowledge and understanding of nature and its sounds. She set to work with enthusiasm, remarking that she would be able to include every imaginative idea that might occur to her, particularly for percussion, for the young players would enjoy the adventure in sound. She was herself as ready as ever for adventure.

84. Coat of arms ot the Worshipful Company of Musicians.

85. Acknowledging applause for *Wildlife (Celebration)*, 1984.

86. Meeting HRH Princess Anne.

The piece was called *Wildlife (Celebration)*, and was dedicated to Yehudi Menuhin and the Jersey Youth Orchestra. She had written in parts for the marimba, but did not discover until the director of the Youth Orchestra received the score, that there was no marimba on the island. At Michael Tippett's suggestion, they achieved the same effect by muting drum sticks and using them to play the strings of the piano. After the concert Priaulx met Princess Anne and was delighted when the Princess immediately remarked upon the cross she was wearing. Her nephew, Peter, had brought it as a gift from Ethiopia, and the Princess, recognizing its provenance, quickly established a dialogue with her.

As her work was always original, always different, it was not surprising that in an interview for *Ideas of Today*, Priaulx was asked how the ordinary listener should approach a piece of modern music. She replied:

> The majority of listeners still wish to have well-tried pegs to hang things on and are not prepared to venture into music with quite different approaches. They should participate more than they do and realise that they have to work to get something worthwhile out of any work of art. If they are willing to listen to a modern work, then they should listen to the *sounds* without preconceived ideas and try to enter the new world that this music is drawing upon. What is this world? Who knows? Most creative artists are prophetic of what is to come, and so cannot fully define what they are about. But they are aware of the changes coming in the developing consciousness of man, they write of things long before their time and the changes they have anticipated come about later.
>
> New forms require new approaches. For instance, early this century the Royal Academy did not allow its students to play Beethoven's late quartets or piano sonatas because they were regarded as outside the field of music. These were astonishingly ahead of their time. They represented a new understanding, a new development of the consciousness of man. Sounds are mere symbols for something deeper. The great creative artist has an awareness beyond the rest of mankind and so it appears that in his work a strange world of sound opens which is not understandable for a while. Before his late work Beethoven's music was concerned with human passions and despairs and jubilation but then he moved into a world of more abstract thought, a more universal sphere.

87. With Michael Tippett, *c.*1984–5.

88. Talking about music.

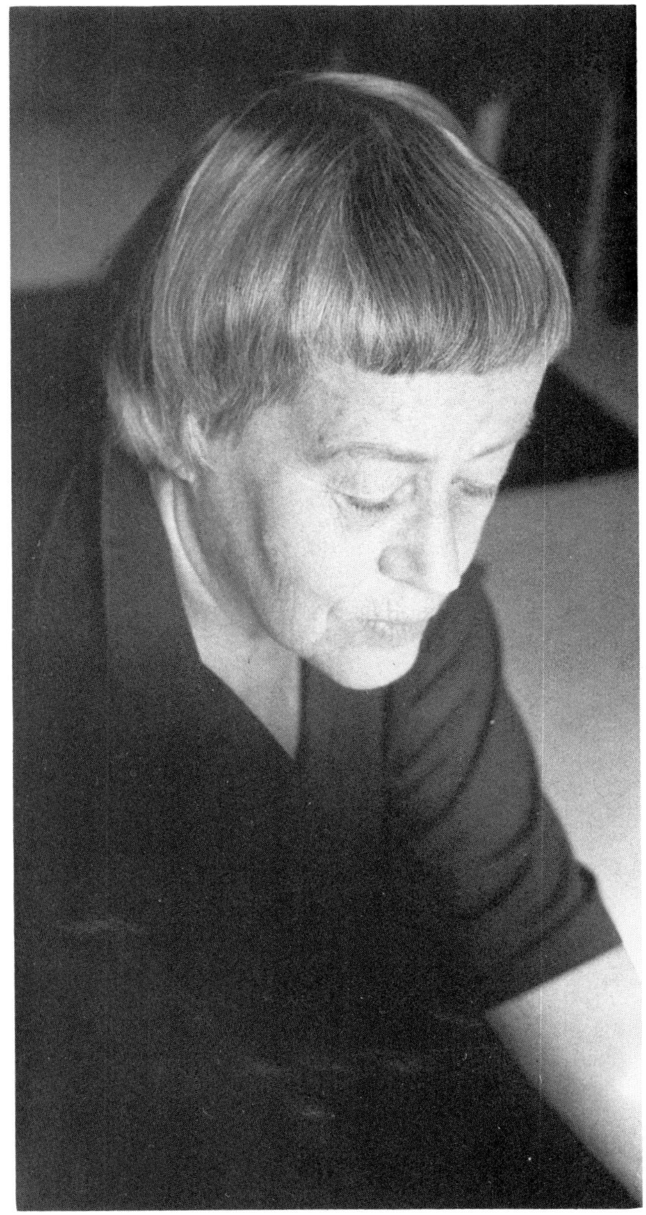

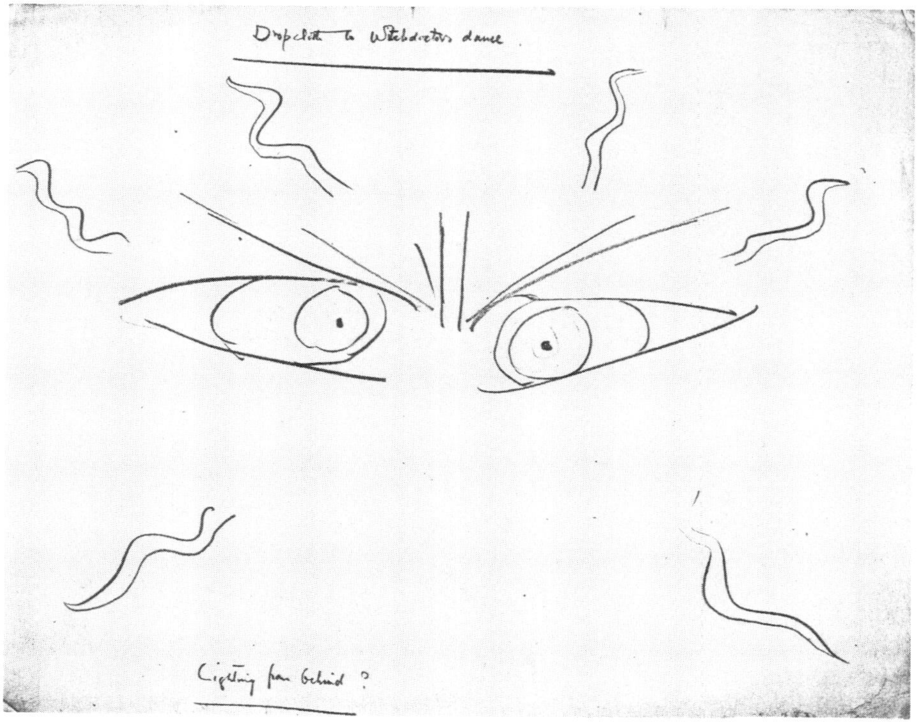

89, 90. Drawings for *The Witchdoctor's Dance*, dropcloth and scene.

> Here it was not so much man that was his subject as an aspect of his consciousness, where consciousness becomes aware of further realities.
>
> In the best works of the great creative artists there is a timelessness and also a sense of continuity which comes from the historical line of development. Such artists are moved by a universal impulse. But these great figures are just as scarce as they have ever been. Geniuses do not rise up all the time.

After *Celebration* Priaulx began to plan a work for the students of the Menuhin School. She looked forward to it with the enthusiasm she always felt when beginning a new work, and without the dread of meeting a deadline because the commission gave her complete freedom to produce what she liked and when.

Also in her mind was an idea for music for a staged production of *The Witchdoctor's Dance*. She had already drawn the entire stage design, backdrop, and positions for lighting; and had written notes on the music for each act and the divisions of the acts. Like Rilke's *Sonnets* she had been thinking about this music for some years, and in 1985 collected together the drawings and notes for *The Witchdoctor's Dance*, and those for the *Sonnets*, saying quietly that perhaps now she was ready for them.

William Glock wrote of Priaulx's continuing eagerness to take risks:

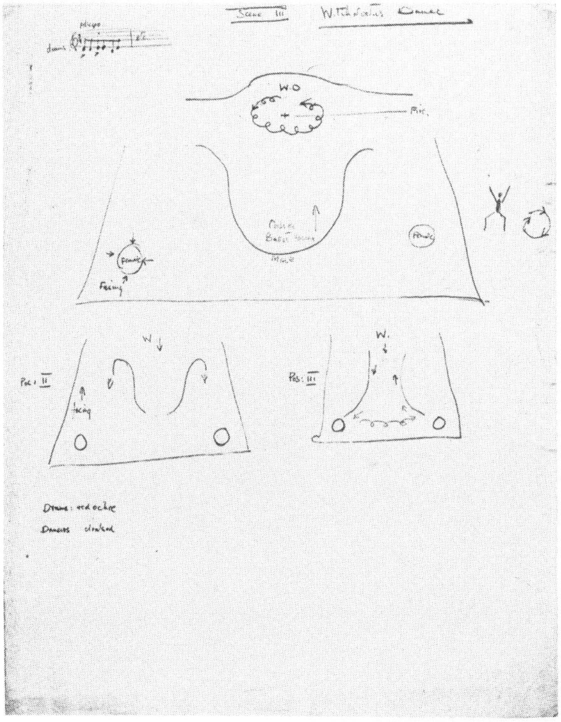

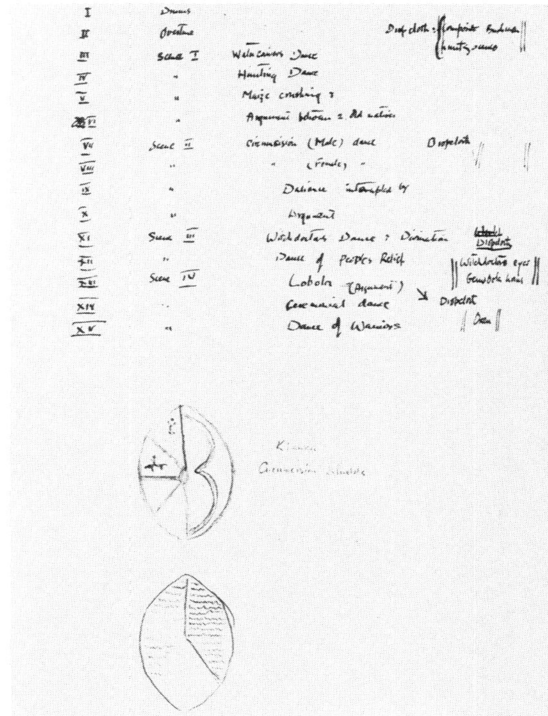

91. Structure of *The Witchdoctor's Dance.*

In 1950 she was working on a cycle of poems by Rilke that she must eventually have abandoned and wrote to me: 'The final scoring is a devil of a task. Do remember, I have to begin with what most people have forgotten. By the time I'm 80 I may wag my head and know something'.

That certainly happened, I think, as one can see by comparing the orchestral writing in the *Duo Concertante* for oboe and clarinet with that of *Aequora Lunae* composed fourteen years earlier. But it is in the chamber music – in *Quanta* and *The Bee Oracles* and the impassioned settings of Devotions by John Donne in *Cycle for Declamation* – that one finds the essence of Priaulx's music. These three works alone cover a remarkable range of expression, because she was always venturing into new territory. Just as her music after its early days seems hardly influenced at all even by those she admired the most so she felt compelled never to repeat herself. More than once in her letters she says how invaluable it is after finishing each work, and before beginning on another, to be able to hear a performance and so move on to 'take more risks, to be more daring'. This refrain may be heard all through her artistic career, right on until the *Grand Duo*, an extraordinary piece to have written at the age of eighty, and showing an energy and audacity of spirit that one imagines in some of her seafaring ancestors of the 17th century.

92. **Philip Langridge, who sang all Priaulx's major works.**

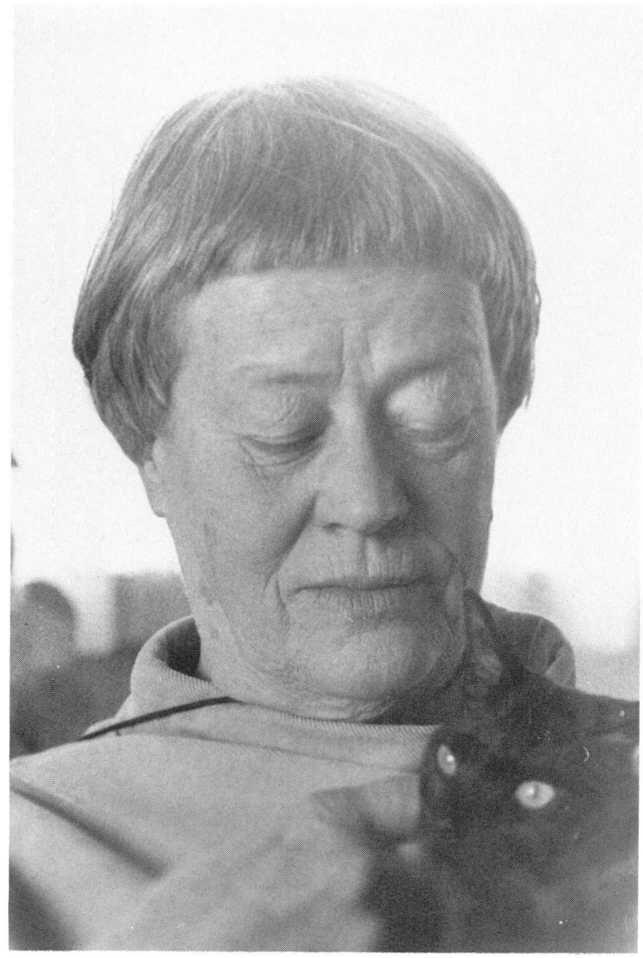

93. **Priaulx with cat.**

Priaulx took Rilke's *Sonnets* and the notes and drawings for *The Witchdoctor's Dance* with her on an autumn holiday in the Auvergne in 1986. At eighty-three she was still longing to write the music for them. She had spent an idyllic two weeks on the mountain slopes, above Besse-en-Chandesse; days of cloudless skies and alpine sun. With a week of the holiday remaining she had mapped out a journey to the highest attainable point, by car, in a chain of extinct volcanoes, near Salers, and decided one morning, after a night brilliant with stars, that it would be an ideal day to go.

94. Cape Point, southernmost tip of Cape Town.

It was frosty and the air was cold, but the sun quickly warmed everything. By midday it was as hot as summer, but the light more brilliant. The route followed a steep, winding road which, as it curved higher and higher, revealed crater after crater, their deep dishes lined with forests so vibrant with autumn colours that they lit the noonday sky. Priaulx left the car several times to absorb and marvel. Eventually the road followed the lip of a crater along its circumference, and in the saddle, where centuries before molten lava had formed a break, a stop was made for lunch.

95. Mount Rainier, Washington, USA, named after Admiral Peter Rainier, an ancestor.

Putting the wine on a flat stone to 'warm in the sun', Priaulx rolled her slacks up to her knees: 'I'm going to listen to the silence', she said, and walked along the crater's edge to stand, hands linked behind her back, head up, listening; feeling the movement of the earth as it rotated on its axis and made its passage around the sun. On the return journey she was unusually silent, and when her attention was called to the play of light in a gorge, said quietly, 'I don't want to look, today has been a perfect experience.'

After an untroubled night's sleep she died, suddenly, before dawn on the morning of 10 October.

Chronological List of Works

1937	*Three Greek Epigrams* for soprano or tenor and piano
1937/9	Piano *Étude*
1939	String Quartet
1943	Suite for Clarinet and Piano
1944	Music for the film *Fire in our Factory*
1945	Sonata for Viola and Piano
1947	*Sinfonia da Camera* for string orchestra
1947	*Dance of the Rain* for tenor or soprano and guitar
1948	*Ubunzima* for tenor or soprano and guitar
1949	*Barbaric Dance Suite* for piano
1950	Ballet Suite for Orchestra (manuscript)
1953	*Cycle for Declamation* for tenor or soprano
1953	Music for the film *Cornwall and the Sculpture of Barbara Hepworth: Figures in a Landscape*
1955	Five Pieces for Keyboard
1955–6	*Requiem* for tenor and a cappella choir
1957	Six Pieces for Five Wind Instruments
1958–9	*Pastoral Triptych* for Solo Oboe
1960	Trio Suite for violin, cello and piano

1960–1	Dance Concerto 'Phala-Phala' for orchestra
1961–2	*Quanta* for oboe and string trio
1963–5	Suite for Solo Cello or Viola
1964	Concerto for Cello and Orchestra
1965–6	String Trio
1966–7	*Aequora Lunae* for orchestra
1969	*The Bee Oracles* for tenor or baritone solo, flute, oboe, violin, cello and harpsichord
1971	*Quinque* for harpsichord
1972	Organ *Gloriana*
1972–3	*Ploërmel* for wind and percussion (material available from the BBC)
1973	*Duo: Vision and Prayer* for tenor and piano
1974	*Primordial Canticles* for organ
1974–6	*Prayers from the Ark* for tenor and harp
1976–7	*Due Canti e Finale* for violin and orchestra
1977–80	*Duo Concertante* for two winds and orchestra
1980–2	*Grand Duo* for cello and piano
1984	*Wildlife (Celebration)* for violin and orchestra

Acknowledgements

The author and publishers would like to thank all those who helped, provided information and lent and collected photographs at such short notice, in particular Dora Begert, Sally Groves and Brian Smith. For permission to reproduce works and photographs we are grateful to: David Addey (36); Akkersdyk Studios, Cape Town (82); BBC (66, 68); Timothy Baxter (26) (photo Frederika Davis); Lady Bliss (66); the Britten-Pears Library (40) (photo Clive Strutt); Nigel Butterley (78) (photo Laurence Le Guay & John Nisbett, Sydney); Michael Craxton (74); EMI (56) (photo Reg Wilson); *Evening Post*, Jersey (86); John Fill (45); David Gascoyne (77) (photo Alain Delaunois); Peter Gellhorn (75, 76) (photos Christopher Davies, Report, London); Roman Grösser (72); Brian Hawkins (54); James Hodge (96); Nicholas Horne (52); Kettle's Yard, University of Cambridge (51, 70) (photos James Austin); Peter Kinnear (69); Philip Langridge (92) (photo Allied Artists); Roger Mayne (34); Susie Mészáros (80) (photo Pic); Miette Muthesius (25); SATOUR (1, 6, 20, 94); Schott (53, 71) (photos Bob Berry); Catharine Scudamore (35); Michael Tippett (31, 87); Felicitas Vogler (50); the Worshipful Company of Musicians (84); the Yehudi Menuhin School (79) (photo Clive Friend).

The publishers have made every effort to trace copyright of photographs, and regret that, in some cases, this has not been possible.

96. The author, June Opie.

The author

June Opie has broadcast and lectured on a wide range of subjects in Europe and New Zealand, and her articles have been published in Europe, Japan, the USA and New Zealand. She knew Priaulx Rainier well for many years.

Published with the aid of a grant from the Priaulx Rainier Memorial Fund (administered by the Worshipful Company of Musicians).